Together We Stand

Queer Elders Speak Out

QUIRK-E
Queer Imaging and Riting Kollective for Elders

Edited by Don Martin and Val Innes

Copyright © 2020 Queer Imaging and Riting Kollective for Elders (Quirk-e).

All rights reserved. No part of this book may be reproduced, stored, or transmitted by any means—whether auditory, graphic, mechanical, or electronic—without written permission of the author, except in the case of brief excerpts used in critical articles and reviews. Unauthorized reproduction of any part of this work is illegal and is punishable by law.

ISBN: 978-1-6847-1854-2 (sc)
ISBN: 978-1-6847-1855-9 (e)

Because of the dynamic nature of the Internet, any web addresses or links contained in this book may have changed since publication and may no longer be valid. The views expressed in this work are solely those of the author and do not necessarily reflect the views of the publisher, and the publisher hereby disclaims any responsibility for them.

Lulu Publishing Services rev. date: 02/27/2020

Together We Stand Queer Elders Speak Out is an unique and amazing book by members of Quirk-e that provides details of how the group organizes and works with original writing in prose, poetry, graphic novel, and playwriting. I laughed, I cried more than once, and I am in awe of the histories of LGBTQ2SIA+ activism recorded here for posterity. This is a book about art and activism, it IS both art and activism. Treasure these words from our queer elders.
—Dr. Jen Marchbank, Professor in Gender,
Sexuality & Women's Studies,
Simon Fraser University, and Co-founder of
the LGBTQ2SIA+ activist group,
Youth 4 A Change

The memoirs are so compelling I started out with the intention of skimming and ended up reading every one. Those in the first section will resonate with anyone who remembers being singled out by a teacher or bullied by classmates because she/he was different.
—Gloria M. Gutman, PhD, FCAHS, LLD
(Hon.), OBC, Professor/Director Emerita,
Department of Gerontology/Gerontology Research Centre,
Simon Fraser University Vancouver Campus

Other Works by Quirk-e

Quirk-e Collected Writings, Volume 1, 2006

Transformations Quirk-e Collected Writings, Volume 2, 2007. Edited and with a preface by Wayson Choy

Outspoken Collected Writings from the Quirk-e Collective, Volume 3, 2008. Edited and with a preface by Wayson Choy

Wrinkles Quirk-e Collected Writings, Volume 4, 2009. Edited by Ria Kim Nishikawara

Quirk-e Collections Writings from the Quirk-e Collective, Volume 5, 2010. Edited by Ria Kim Nishikawara

The Bridge Generation A queer elders' chronicle from no rights to civil rights, 2014. Edited by Claire Robson and Kelsey Blair

LGBTQ Elder Abuse: What do you know?, 2015. Video PSA and poster project on financial, emotional, sexual, and physical abuse of LGBTQ elders

Basically Queer An Intergenerational Introduction to LGBTQA2S+ Lives, 2017. Edited by Claire Robson, Kelsey Blair, and Jen Marchbank

This Patch of Grass on Which I Stand, A Zine by the Memoir Writing Group, 2018.

To contact us write to:
Quirk-e
Britannia Community Services Centre
1661 Napier Street, Vancouver, BC V5L 4X4
Canada

Dedicated to Wayson Choy
1939 – 2019

To us in Quirk-e, Wayson was a gift, a generous and kind-hearted man, a writer who encouraged us, a mentor who read our books and commented thoughtfully, praised us, and embraced our mission to write our queer stories. We will miss him.

Wayson Choy was a pioneer of Asian Canadian literature and an openly gay writer of colour. Author of *The Jade Peony, Paper Shadows: A Chinatown Childhood, All That Matters* and *Not Yet: A Memoir of Living and Almost Dying*, Wayson won numerous awards including the Trillium Book Award, the George Woodcock Lifetime Achievement Award, and membership in The Order of Canada.

In The Beginning . . .
Judy Fletcher

CONTENTS

ACKNOWLEDGMENTS xi
FOREWORD Val Innes xiii
HOW QUIRK-E WORKS Don Martin xvii

Section 1: MEMOIR 1
   Memoir Writing Group Process Cyndia Cole 1
   Guest Artist Workshop Claire Robson 6
   Lessons Learned Val Innes 8
   Nearly High Noon Judy Fletcher 10
   Hebrew School and Stealing Lessons 1951 Marsha Ablowitz 13
   Ne T'en Fais Pas [Do Not Worry] Farren Gillaspie 20
   A Failure of Democracy Ellen Woodsworth 23
   My Early Years in School Greta Hurst 28
   Death Equals Silence Chris Morrissey 31
   A More Masculine Pursuit Don Martin 35
   Library Day River Glen 39
   Mickey and the Martian Farren Gillaspie 42
   Unintended Consequences Janie Cawley 44
   True Religion Cyndia Cole 49
   Parents' Walk About Gayle Roberts 52
   All My Art Schools Nancy Strider 55

   A DIALOGUE IN FOUR PARTS 62
   Child's Play Gayle Roberts 63
   Who Knew? Cyndia Cole 65
   Too Much Lari Souza 66
   Generations Richard Brail 67

MORE MEMOIR Val Innes 71
An Early Fall Stephen Hardy 72
Thanksgiving Chef Don Martin..76
Working Day Blues River Glen 82
Grandpa John: Simple Treasures Pat Hogan........................ 84
Not the Right Time Harris Taylor.. 87
My Femininity Lari Souza... 89
**Awareness and Love—Shame, Blame and
Resentment** Farren Gillaspie.. 91
Getting Old Greta Hurst 93
Aging Out Val Innes.. 95

Section 2: GRAPHIC MEMOIR 97
Graphic Memoir Group Process Judy Fletcher with
Val Innes 97
Guest Artist Workshop Sarah Leavitt....................................... 99

MESSAGES RECEIVED AND INTERNALIZED 101
Child Judy Fletcher...101
Teen Chris Morrissey 102
Younger Senior Anonymous QUIRK-E....................................103
Senior Chris Morrissey...104

MORE COMIC STORIES 105
Good Feet Cyndia Cole..105
New School Judy Fletcher 106
So There! Judy Fletcher...107
Christmas Presents Cyndia Cole 108
Tommy Judy Fletcher..109
Fears Judy Fletcher..110

Section 3: PLAYWRITING.. 111
Playwriting Group Process Don Martin and Val Innes......111
Guest Artist Workshop Dorothy Dittrich...............................114
Script of "A Chorus Line of Characters" 116

Section 4: TRAVELS WITH QUIRK-E Val Innes 121
   Patted Down Sheila Gilhooly... 122
   It's Customary Chris Morrissey 126
   Spain: Famed Trans Singer, Falete Paula Stromberg 129
   The Resurrection Marsha Ablowitz.......................................132
   Melaque, Mexico Cyndia Cole 136
   Fishing Chris Morrisey..139
   Peace Val Innes 143
   Arctic Adventure Harris Taylor 144
   Morning in Glen Park Nora D Randall 145

Section 5: TOGETHER WE STAND Val Innes........................147
   You Have Struck a Rock Ellen Woodsworth.......................148
   I Support That River Glen..150
   Socializing the Problem Chris Morrissey.............................153
   Working from the Inside Farren Gillaspie............................158
   I'm Here with You Cyndia Cole 161
   If I Had a Hammer: Remembering Christopher Colorado Jones, 70 Don Martin 166

QUIRK-E AUTHORS **171**
GUEST ARTISTS.. **177**

LIST OF ADDITIONAL ILLUSTRATIONS
   In The Beginning . . . Judy Fletcher... vi
   Different Schools Judy Fletcher.. 5
   Dancing Bear Judy Fletcher 61
   A Soft Place To Land Judy Fletcher 125

ACKNOWLEDGMENTS

Quirk-e would like to acknowledge the Britannia Community Services Centre staff and administration for its ongoing support over the years. Britannia has been our home for the last thirteen years, and we're very grateful for the welcome and support we receive there, particularly from Anne Cowan, senior services programmer, who continues to guide and look out for us. We would also like to acknowledge QMUNITY, Vancouver's LGBTQ2S+ resource centre, for the support they have given us and the work they do in the community.

We are very grateful for the City of Vancouver Community Arts Grant Program which has funded this anthology and our workshops. Their support made the anthology, the play, and the workshops possible. The Roundhouse Community Arts and Recreation Centre co-sponsored our playwriting workshop and offered us the use of their theatre. They also host the Senior Arts and Health Showcase each year, which is sponsored by Vancouver Coastal Health and Vancouver Board of Parks and Recreation, and offers us an opportunity to present our work to their audience.

We offer deeply-felt, special thanks to guest artists Claire Robson, Dorothy Dittrich, Sarah Leavitt, and Lorna Boschman for leading our workshops on memoir, playwriting, comic storytelling, and video storytelling, and for offering their ongoing support. What a joy and privilege it is to work with these talented women.

Paula Stromberg, Marsha Ablowitz, John Konovsky, Richard Brail, Harris Taylor, and Val Innes contributed photographs; Judy Fletcher, Harris Taylor, Don Martin, and Cyndia Cole helped prepare art files; Dennis Sumara hosted a discussion on Prime Minister Trudeau's apology to the LGBTQ2S community that helped advance our work on the play; Carla White designed our cover; and Lulu Publishing formatted and printed the book. Thank you all for your hard work. Thanks, of course, to all the members of Quirk-e for submitting their wonderful stories to this book and for being willing to accept edits. A special thanks to Judy Fletcher whose drawings appear in both the Graphic Memoir section and scattered throughout this book.

Finally, we would like to acknowledge Wayson Choy, to whom we have dedicated this book. Despite his busy life as one of Canada's best-known authors, Wayson had agreed to read and endorse this anthology. He was an ally, friend, and mentor since 2006 right up to his death in 2019, before we were able to finish the manuscript.

FOREWORD
Val Innes

The Queer Imaging and Riting Kollective for Elders (Quirk-e) in Vancouver, British Columbia, is a collective of twenty-two queer (LGBTQA2S+) artists. Most of us have been political and cultural activists since the '60s and '70s and continue to advocate for justice and social change today. We lived through times when homosexuality and gender variance were defined first as crimes and then mental disorders. We started in the 'closet', hiding for fear of losing jobs, family, and friends. When we 'came out' we were often subjected to rejection, discrimination, bullying, and violence. Our histories and herstories as activists, artists, and writers reflect our lifelong struggles for dignity and human rights. We work in written and spoken word, in theatre, memoir, video, graphic arts, and photographs. We have published six anthologies and a textbook, with Youth for a Change, titled ***Basically Queer*** *An Intergenerational Introduction to LGBTQA2S+ Lives* (Peter Lang, 2017). Over the years, in addition to books, we have done visual art pieces, multimedia presentations, public service announcements, and periodic open mic performances. We are regularly asked to read our essays, poems, and short stories at community events. Our collaborative work with queer youth about LGBTQA2S+ elder abuse has been presented widely in B.C.

Quirk-e was founded by Chris Morrissey and Claire Robson in 2006 when they brought together a group of queer elders interested in writing their memoirs. That group held four workshop sessions called Writing Our LGBT Lives, led by Claire. As Claire noted in 2017, in one of our previous anthologies, ***The Bridge Generation***, Quirk-e began as

> a happy coincidence. I was new to town and looking to network. Chris Morrissey was in charge of programming at the Generations Project. We put together a series of workshops at the old 411 Senior Centre on Dunsmuir Street in Vancouver.
>
> How quickly things got out of hand!
>
> By the end of six weeks, the group had begun to morph into a band of *artivists*—artist activists writing back to stereotypes about being old and queer. Instead of being an in-charge writing teacher, I had become more like a pirate captain—negotiating precarious consensus among a band of opinionated peers. When it came to the final session, my 'students' refused to go away.

Claire goes on to describe how, in a stroke of sheer ingenuity, Chris brokered the writing group's acceptance into the Senior Arts and Health Collaborative—a pilot project managed by Vancouver Board of Parks and Recreation and Vancouver Coastal Health.

> Thanks to their commitment to free long-term arts experiences for seniors, we had three years of support and funding—a treat for a generation used to meeting in church basements and friends' living rooms. In these three luxurious years, we coined our name, revised our mission, and invented brand new ways of working together.

Britannia Community Services Centre donated a meeting space and eventually Quirk-e became one of their regular programs with the support of seniors programmer Anne Cowan. The Generations Project was part of what is now called Qmunity, B.C.'s queer, trans and two-spirit resource centre, and Qmunity remains a valued community partner. They still provide us with a small annual grant for weekly snacks and include readings by our members at many of their regular events.

For a decade Claire was the lead artist for Quirk-e. She was an adjunct faculty member at Simon Fraser University, so Quirk-e also established strong ties to academia. Claire was aided by a series of co-hosts and volunteers, including Nancy Strider, Ria Nishikiwara, Shelley Whitehead, and Kelsey Blair. During her tenure Claire said, we

> work with images, text, and performance to make art that notices everything—the sags and wrinkles, the moments of grace, the beautiful and the absurd. We remain constantly precarious—a discordant choir that welcomes differences, conflicts, and irreconcilable points of view. And we remain activists, ready and able to point out inequality and tackle it.

With Claire's departure in 2017, after years of her planning and facilitating our weekly meetings, Quirk-e became a true collective, establishing a co-ordinating committee of five members—Cyndia Cole, Pat Hogan, Val Innes, Don Martin, and Chris Morrisey. We also engaged a youth volunteer, Lari Souza, to help us with various organizational tasks, and he has now become an active member of our group.

Quirk-e has a particular history, set in a city that, for the most part, is friendly to queers. Yet what we have done can be replicated elsewhere. If you want to have a group like this, you can do it, and it's worth doing. It takes one or two people to have the vision and pursue it. You can start in a home, a library, a room in a nearby community centre or college, or in a queer centre, if you're lucky enough to live in a community that has one. You can apply for grants or solicit small donations; you can have an artistic lead, or a small group of facilitators, but you can make this happen. If you love writing or creating plays or working with images, starting a queer seniors' group where you can share this love with other like-minded people may be just the thing for you.

And we are here to tell you how we do it. In this anthology, we're setting out some of our process, and making more of our stories public. This is history we're sharing, and it's a history/herstory that has long been silenced. Here's your chance to join in the telling, as well as building a group that will have your back no matter what happens to you. We've seen each other through major life changes, as you'll see when you read some of the stories or poems in here; some of them have been easy changes, some hard. A few of us have died, some have been ill, some have become grandparents, some have entered or left relationships, some have retired, and some have taken on leadership responsibilities. New members have joined just in the past few years, months, or even weeks, but a constant has been our weekly meetings, our writing, our sharing, our politics, and our interest in each other's lives throughout the years.

There is still plenty of work to do. Trans folks have only recently gained civil rights; homophobia and transphobia continue to plague us, as does verbal and physical violence, even though for the majority of Canadians, acceptance is far more the norm than it ever has been. Positive changes are due largely to the gay and lesbian liberation movement of which we are all a part. By sharing our experiences, we can help future generations of LGBTQA2S+ people achieve and maintain our rightful place in society.

HOW QUIRK-E WORKS
Don Martin

Quirk-e meets every Wednesday for two hours at Britannia Community Services Centre in Vancouver's Grandview-Woodland neighbourhood along Commercial Drive. Our season runs from September through June. We don't meet in July and August or on holidays. Since the fall of 2017, Quirk-e, true to its name, has managed itself as a collective. Our artistic leadership is handled by a five-member coordinating committee which facilitates the planning of yearly activities, rotates the weekly chore of running meetings, and performs other administrative functions. We decided on a five-member committee to avoid tie votes and to ensure there were enough people to cover absences due to illness or travel. All of the committee members have backgrounds in writing, design, performance, and organizational support. The coordinating committee makes operational recommendations. Decisions are made by the whole membership through consensus after thorough discussion. To us consensus means: I don't have to love it, but I'm able to live with it.

In our first season under collective management (2017-2018), each of our members self-selected one of four smaller groups to participate in: memoir writing, playwriting, graphic storytelling, and video storytelling. We engaged four local artists in these genres to conduct two-hour workshops as a kick-off to the season. The guest artists were Claire Robson (memoir), Dorothy Dittrich (playwriting), Sarah Leavitt (graphic storytelling), and Lorna Boschman (video storytelling). These workshops were energizing, inspirational, and reflected the esteem in which Vancouver's arts community holds our group. Sometime in the winter, the video production small group, which had only three members and faced technical challenges, decided to dissolve and be absorbed into the other three small groups. Our broad theme for the year was *This Patch of Grass on Which I Stand*, which we used as a writing prompt and a focus for exploring our role as queer elders in the community.

In our 2018-2019 season Quirk-e applied for and received a $6500 Community Arts Grant from the City of Vancouver to continue the work of the small groups. The purpose of the grant was to engage local artists in community-based projects. We expanded on our previous year's experience and invited three of the guest artists back to lead half-day workshops open to the whole community.

Since 2006, Quirk-e has participated in the Senior Arts and Health collaborative, an initiative to promote healthy aging through arts programming and community engagement. Arts and Health, jointly sponsored by the Vancouver Board of Parks and Recreation and Vancouver Coastal Health, produces a showcase each spring of performances and exhibits by seniors from participating community centres in the city. The showcase features a range of arts activities from writing and visual arts, to dance, singing, weaving, cedar hat making, puppetry, and gardening. Each group is led by a professional artist, many of whom focus on traditional ethnic or cultural practices. At the annual Arts and Health Showcase in June 2018, Quirk-e presented:

- A 10-minute skit with six actors dramatizing our playwriting process
- An exhibit of sketches illustrating the process of the graphics group
- A compilation video produced during our kick-off workshop on video production
- A reading by one of the memoir group participants along with printed copies of the memoir group's 20-page zine.

Quirk-e's contributions to the June 2019 Arts and Health Showcase are included in this self-published anthology, a compilation of the work of our small groups plus additional writing and images our members produced during the past year. This anthology is also partially funded by the Community Arts Grant from the City of Vancouver.

Section 1:
MEMOIR

Memoir Writing Group Process
Cyndia Cole

Quirk-e's Memoir Writing Group was created in the fall of 2017. We agreed that we would support each other to work on individual pieces rather than trying to co-write collective work. Our numbers have varied, and about eight members is usual. Some of us are working toward book-length memoirs. As of June 2019, one of these is complete and has been accepted for publication, and another is close to being a finished manuscript. Other group participants are happy to be writing shorter pieces. One strength of our format has been the ability to continue as our membership changes—some leaving due to health or personal reasons, new folks joining. In addition, people can participate through email even when travelling, caring for a sick friend in another city, or attending conferences abroad.

In June of 2018, we self-published a 20-page Zine entitled *This Patch of Grass on Which I Stand*. Each of us in the Memoir Writing Group contributed two pages of stories or poems. We also created photos and graphics to illustrate our theme. We printed two hundred copies on paper of differing colours to give a rainbow effect. At the yearly Seniors Arts and Health Showcase, we distributed one hundred copies for free to a mostly heterosexual, cis-gender audience. The other hundred copies went quickly to our queer friends and allies. We agreed to distribute free e-copies of the Zine upon request. To keep up with the demand, one of our supporters had another fifty copies printed for use by both queer elder and youth groups.

We kicked off Quirk-e's 2018-19 season with a four-hour workshop called *You've Got A Story to Tell!* Guest artist, and former Quirk-e lead artist, Claire Robson helped us understand differences between memoir and autobiography. Claire also challenged us to examine the lessons learned in and out of school when we formed our life shaping values. Following the workshop, those in the memoir group crafted our stories using the critique process below.

At the June 2019 Seniors Arts and Health Showcase we performed the pieces published here in *Dialogue in Four Parts*. The dialogue began with the poem by Lari Souza, our youth volunteer. Using it as a writing prompt, Richard Brail, Gayle Roberts and Cyndia Cole added in their own voices on the theme of 'wanting too much'. Paula Stromberg captured expressive portraits which give faces to these voices.

Central to the memoir writing group's process is the use of Quirk-e's Contract for Critique which we created in 2012, discussed and refined several times since.

CONTRACT FOR CRITIQUE:

- *Speak to the intention. Start with the big picture rather than being picky.*
- *Invite amplification. Say where you need more information, or where you are confused.*
- *Read carefully. Respect the work. Be an advocate for it.*
- *It's not about you. Don't score points. Don't try to rewrite the work for the author.*
- *Lead with the strengths. But be honest about the weaknesses. Indicate those places where you were confused or uncomfortable.*
- *Try always to strengthen the work—to make it what it wants to be.*
- *Separate the author from the work. Don't assume that the work reflects his/her opinions or that it is autobiographical. Don't direct criticism at the author.*

- *Respect the values and perspective of the piece. Let go of judgments. It doesn't matter what YOU like—what does the work want?*
- *Say SOMETHING. Silence can unsettle. At the very least, you can feed back words or phrases or images that you liked.*

At times, we email the pieces we're working on to the others in the group and ask for critique by email response. At times, we email the piece and wait for critique during our small group time at Quirk-e meetings. At times, we read our piece out during the small group and listen to critique on the spot. After we edit the piece based on critique, we may be open to further comment or not; we choose. Some of us find scheduling a consistent time for writing helps us get down to it. Some of us wish we spent more time writing during the group meetings.

Despite the wise guidelines in the Contract for Critique, it's not an easy process. It can be difficult to give and to receive. Our goal is to encourage each other to keep writing, to write more and to write better, but sometimes, even with the best of intentions, giving and receiving of critiques may go awry. If someone is deviating from the Contract for Critique, the person chairing the session has a responsibility to keep members from going off track. If the critique is done in pairs, each person is responsible to inform their partner if they are going off track. Each of us has self responsibility. If you'd like to use this tool, please use it with care.

We are all vulnerable about our writing abilities. And our subject, by definition, is very personal. During our lives, our voices and stories often were silenced by shame, stigma or fear of consequences for speaking out. If we experience the critique as insensitive, overwhelming, off base or just plain not helpful, instead of writing more and better we may just stop ourselves. When this happens, we try to communicate respectfully and truthfully. We return to the Contract for Critique, return to focus on the intention of the work, return to our intention to help each other. As writers, we keep faith in our own creative compass. Other people's comments are just opinion—and we ourselves know best about the value and direction of our own creative work.

Most of the time the Memoir Writing Group process works as long-awaited acknowledgment. We engage with the other members in a way that empowers us. We are excited, nourished, and uplifted by saying what needs to be said. We are eager and proud to attend Quirk-e readings in the community. Communicating with elders and across generations is fulfilling our mission to share our unique LGBTQIA2S lives and, in doing so, we hold up a lamp that may light the way for others.

Different Schools
Judy Fletcher

Guest Artist Workshop:
Lessons Learned
Claire Robson

The lessons we learn in school don't just involve the ABCs, but include what is required of men and women, what is considered 'normal' and what is forbidden. For those of us who are different, in terms of race, colour, physical appearance, temperament ability, gender, and sexual identifications, these lessons can be radically at odds with our desires, our lived experience of the world, and what we feel and know to be right. And that pretty much includes everyone. Almost every fish in the schools of fish that swim from classroom to classroom feels out of place at some point and in some way. Of course, for those who are counter-normative in terms of gender and sexuality, it can be particularly difficult and confusing.

Our schools offer a place where social norms and our feelings and desires collide, and at a particularly sensitive time in our lives. Though we can make friends and have fun at school, we can also lose our innocence, endure hurt, and learn things that were never meant to be on the curriculum. When I was invited to offer a writing workshop by the coordinators of Quirk-e, this was the topic I decided would be rich in material to explore. The workshop (made possible by a grant from the City of Vancouver) was held in the Family Education Centre at Britannia Community Services Centre on September 19, 2018 and open to members of the public.

We began with a simple mapping exercise, in order to remind us of the physical realities of the school spaces we inhabited. Sometimes, memoir writing can focus too narrowly upon individual emotional responses, and thus become too generalized and internal. It is when we recall the realities of the scene—the face of the teacher, the size of her desk, the sound of the bell—that the writing comes to life for the reader. We wrote all morning about our maps and the memories they generated, then spent the afternoon sharing our work with others and revising it using the feedback offered.

We hope that you enjoy the results!

Lessons Learned
Val Innes

You have to play nice
but if others don't, that's ok in Canada,
but not in Scotland. A prefect will stop you.
Lesson learned.

In Aberdeen, I had a pet mouse, and I took it to school,
hid her in my desk.
The teacher saw and let me show her to
all the class; it became a lesson:
we take care of our pets and don't frighten them. Lesson learned.

You should do all your homework as soon as you can
but lots of kids don't, and, in Canada, nothing happens;
it did in Scotland.
You should fit in and wear the right clothes,
because they don't wear uniforms here,
and if you don't fit in, you suffer:
little Scottish kid with the accent, in the kilt and tie . . .
but . . . you can be "other" and survive that. Lesson learned.

Teachers get off with anything here;
one of them throws wooden blackboard erasers
at kids who don't know the answers.
That's assault.
Another makes the Jewish kids read from the New Testament.
That's cruel.
Another makes us exercise to increase our bust size.
That's weird.

Some teachers do care about kids; that's really nice . . .
though rare.

In art, I got to paint what I wanted when I wanted;
I waited for art all day twice a week. I learned I loved it.
I still paint. I still love it.
In math, I spent every class scared I'd forget and get hit;
I never did, but I learned to hate it
until, as an adult, I built things . . .
I still don't like it, but I use it.
Lessons learned.

Somewhere in there I learned to like bits of school
enough to get me into university four degrees worth,
and I became a teacher.
Lesson:
Get an education. Be an education. Make a difference.
Don't be what you didn't like. Care.

Nearly High Noon
Judy Fletcher

Our family has moved to another farm a few miles outside of Colborne, a small town near Lake Ontario. This is our third move in three years. The teacher at this one-room school is Mr. Pratt, who is just out of normal school they say. This is his first year of teaching. He is pale, with blond hair and a soft voice. He blushes easily. He wears a crisp, white shirt and a tie every day, whereas our dads do that only on Sundays. I am pretty sure that I am not the only girl who has a crush on him.

It's almost lunch time, so no one is really listening as Mr. Pratt reads from the social studies textbook. The younger kids practice their times tables in the corner, and the little ones are copying the alphabet into their scribblers, over and over again.

As teachers before him had, Mr. Pratt mostly ignores the 'big boys in the back of the room'. In rural Ontario, boys have to work on the farm in the spring for planting and in the fall for harvesting. Their parents want them out of the house in the winter, and so they plonk themselves down in the back row of the nearest one-room school. At P.S. 21, we are stuck with the Stickly brothers, three of them. They aren't here to learn. Everyone knows that. Even the enthusiastic Mr. Pratt gave up talking to them after a couple of weeks.

The notorious Stickly family is known all over the county. Their kids are very nearly feral. The oldest of these is Billy Stickly. The bigger boys are supposed to bring the firewood in from the shed out back and keep the fire going in the stove. It has been snowing for days and the schoolroom is cold. But Billy totally ignores the shortage of firewood and leans his head against the back wall and sleeps for most of the day. At this point it is unclear how old Billy is.

For that matter, it is unclear what grade he's in. I don't think anyone cares as long as he's quiet.

I am in Grade 7 in 1956, but I can easily be mistaken for one of the little kids. In these eight-grades-in-one-room schools, I always sit in the front row near the teacher's desk. It is more for protection than for any other reason. I stay nearby at recess to avoid the bullies on the playground. Of course, I want to be near Mr. Pratt as well. I feel safe with Mr. Pratt. Mr. Pratt is our hero, our very own Gary Cooper, like the sheriff in *High Noon*! The movie is our favourite. We girls all fancy ourselves as the incredibly beautiful Grace Kelly. Each of us thinks that, after school today, we will put on our bonnets, climb into the buggy, and ride off into the sunset with Mr. Pratt.

Unfortunately, Billy is awake. He and his brothers are squabbling and cursing about something, or more likely, nothing. Finally, Mr. Pratt lets his frustration with the noise coming from the back boil over, and he lowers the book and yells, "Billy, shut up!" It doesn't work. He slams the book down on his desk. The sound makes us all jump. From the bottom drawer, he retrieves the leather strap that all the country schools are equipped with. The strap is made from two strips of harness leather glued together back to back. It makes a terrifying weapon—one inch thick, four inches wide, and about fifteen inches long. The loud whooshing noise that it makes as it is swung through the air is usually enough to bring order to the room. Not today. The teacher slams it down on his desk. We all stop what we were doing and turn towards the back of the room. Billy is paying attention now. We all are. It is High Noon and every kid in the room is on High Alert.

I hold my breath. My heart's pounding so loud that I think everyone can hear it. I try to not wet my pants. We are all watching with anticipation as if Mr. Pratt is the sheriff, and Billy and his brothers are all the bad guys rolled into one…Billy the Kids! Our 'hero' arrives at the back of the room with the strap dangling by his side. The wooden, two-piece desk bolted to the floor is not made to fit Billy, and with much scraping and banging and moaning and groaning, he begins to untangle himself from it. After what seems like several minutes he is standing. To my left, a little girl starts to whimper. Billy is bigger, taller, and obviously stronger than our heroic teacher. He looks down at Mr. Pratt and raises his closed fist. Mr. Pratt's face turns scarlet. The silence grows deeper, and the sunlight is gone from the room. The only sound is the little girl, crying now. I hold my breath. And I try not to wet my pants. A dog barks in the distance.

Our beloved teacher stares up at Billy. Seconds, minutes crawl past. Billy turns and grins at his brothers. Bobby and Jack pound their desks in glee. Another dog barks in the distance.

Clearly shaken by the situation that he finds himself in, our hero looks away and slowly walks back to the front of the room. He stands very still for a few minutes. Mr. Pratt returns the strap to the desk drawer. Billy Stickly folds himself back into the child's desk and his head falls against the wall in his usual resting pose. The dust settles. All of us begin to breathe again. The little ones return to copying the alphabet; the younger ones do their times tables. The dogs are quiet. The snow piles up against the windows.

In a voice shaking only a little, Mr. Pratt resumes reading the social studies book where he had left off. We are all shaken. With broken hearts, we turn our faces to our books.

No one feels like riding off into the sunset today.

Hebrew School and Stealing Lessons 1951
Marsha Ablowitz

When I was five, Mommy was excited because a new Hebrew day school was opening in Vancouver. I was just turned five and not old enough for English school, but the Hebrew school was looking for more kids, and I could read, so Mommy thought I was ready. The school was square and white with a gravel playground. The first day, all the kids were running and yelling in the playground and throwing the gravel around. Ronnie Balovsky said, "You aren't allowed t' throw rocks."

I said, "Why not?" And since lots of other kids were having fun throwing rocks, I picked one up and threw it. It hit Ronnie in the side of his head. He looked surprised, and his head started bleeding, and tears ran down his cheeks.

"You are in trouble," he said. The monitor took Ronnie to the nurse and told all of us not to throw rocks. We went to our desks.

I started to learn Hebrew. It went from right to left, and English went from left to right, so it was confusing. We had Hebrew in the morning and English in the afternoon. I had hay fever, and my nose ran so much my eyes got blurry. I loved the teacher in her bright red dress. It was easier to read stories in English. I always had my nose in a book. The problem was I had to ride the school bus to Talmud Torah Hebrew Day School every day. I got bus sick.

That summer, I went to Jewish summer camp. I had fun dancing and swimming and eating Cracker Jacks. Then I turned six and was sneezing all the time. My red nose hurt. But I didn't pay attention to my sore nose because it was time for school, and I was busy trying to make a deal with Mommy and Daddy about what school I wanted. I hated riding the bus every day to Talmud Torah. I got so bored stuck inside the bus. Big kids teased me, and the bus driver told me not to drop used Kleenex out of my stuffed pockets.

"Please Mom, I don't wanna go to Hebrew school."

"You need to be with the Jewish kids."

"Please let me go to English school. I get sick on the bus." Finally, Mommy and Daddy said yes, I could drop out of Talmud Torah and walk to a neighbourhood school, but only if I'd go to Beth Israel Hebrew School after school three times a week.

"That way you'll be with Jewish kids," Mommy said.

"Okay, Mommy." The good part was I'd only had to ride to Beth Israel twice a week and once on Sunday morning, and instead of sneezing on the terrible school bus, Mommy and Daddy would drive me to Beth Israel in our car and give me treats. The English school, Queen Elizabeth, was one mile away. Mom thought that was too far for me to walk because I was puny with allergies and asthma. Just one block away was Our Ladies of Perpetual Help, the Catholic school. I really didn't want to go there. The kids wore uniforms and were snobby. The nuns wore gigantic black robes and black and white things on their heads, so you couldn't even see their hair. They were scary.

"Mommy, I don't wanna go to Our Ladies."

"But Marsha, it's so close."

"I'm scared of the nuns."

"Don't you remember the nice nuns when you were in the hospital?" All I remembered from the hospital was that I couldn't breathe in the oxygen tent, and Mommy brought me a little Christmas tree with golden balls. I liked looking at the little tree from the window of my oxygen tent, but Mommy had to take the golden tree away because grandma was coming to see me, and grandma didn't believe in Christmas trees. And then the nun gave me a shiny gold plastic cross, but I had to give it back because we are Jewish.

"Mommy, I'm scared t'cross Tenth Avenue to get to Our Ladies with all the cars going so fast."

"Okay you can go to Queen Elizabeth," she said. At Queen Elizabeth, they couldn't decide what grade to put me into. Since I had just turned six, I should be in Grade 1. But I had finished Grade 1 at Talmud Torah, so they decided to try me in Grade 2. The principal scheduled me for I.Q. tests with a blonde lady who asked me lots of questions and said I was reading at a Grade 6 level. So, they let me stay in Grade 2. Queen Elizabeth School was okay. It had grass outside and trees. I didn't know any kids there, but I loved walking to school especially wading in the mud puddles and picking up coloured rocks in the lane.

The first day of school, I was eating my peanut butter and honey sandwich outside on the grass. A bee came toward me buzzing in the clover. I threw a pebble at him to scare him away from my sandwich. Mary saw me. "You can't throw stones," she said.

I said, "It's not a stone, just a pebble. And it's okay to throw a little pebble at the bee or at your shoe. It won't hurt you." And I threw a tiny pebble and hit her shoe. She ran to tell on me. The monitor took me to the principal's dark office.

"Is this true? Did you throw a stone?" he asked.

"Yes, but it was just a pebble, and it just hit her shoe."

"Put out your hands." he said. When I put out my hands he lifted his arm back and swished something big and brown through the air towards my hands. Quickly I pulled my hands back, and the brown thing hit his leg.

"What's that?" I asked.

"The strap," he said. "Do you know why I asked you to put your hands up?"

"T'see if they were clean?" I guessed. He just laughed and told me to go back to my class.

The teachers at Queen Elizabeth were serious and strict. Not like the teachers after school at the Beth Israel Hebrew School. The afterschool kids called it the B.I., and since it was after regular school, none of the kids wanted to sit still. Everyone was running around. It was way more exciting than English school and much noisier. Paper airplanes, chalk, even books went flying through the air. You had to duck. And kids were jumping and singing and fighting right in the classroom. "Why doesn't the teacher stop them?" I asked Paul sitting in front of me.

"He's not a real teacher," Paul said.

"He's my cousin," I said. Our teacher, Mr. Yorkston, really was my cousin. He just asked us to be quiet and gave us little Jersey milk chocolate squares. Some kids joked about what he did to the older girls in the back room, but he was always nice to me. My desk was spilling out damp Kleenexes, but he didn't mind. Since I already knew the Hebrew alphabet and the prayers from last year at Talmud Torah, I amused myself reading our textbook on Jewish history starting with "In the beginning God created the Heavens and the Earth" . . . and then the garden and Adam . . . and then our forefather Abraham and all his sons. But when I had finished reading the whole history textbook, I got bored. So Mr. Yorkston gave me permission to go by myself down the hall to the library. It was dark and cool and quiet in the library room, books piled all over the place, and because I was alone, I could blow my nose and cough as much as I wanted.

I found a wonderful pile of Jewish history comic books. The first comic I read was the story of Dr. Jonas Salk who discovered a vaccine to cure polio. If my friend from Haro Street, Davy Armstrong, had got that medicine, his arm would not have stopped working, and he could have climbed trees with me. The next comic was about Hannah Senesh, a Jewish heroine killed by the Nazis. She left Hungary after high school and went to be a pioneer in Palestine. But World War II started, and the British rulers said if she parachuted back into Hungary and spied with them, they would help her save some Jewish kids from the death camps. Hannah thought that was a good deal, and she saved kids and saved British airmen until she got caught. She wouldn't tell the Nazis anything even when they tortured her. So, they shot her. She wrote a sad little poem called *Blessed Is the Match*. She was a lady hero. I wanted to be brave like her.

"Mommy, why did nobody rescue us?"

"We heard the terrible stories about the concentration camps, but we couldn't believe that they were true," she said. What was a concentration camp? I returned to the B.I. library and read everything I could find: six million Jews—how many was that?—and all those other people . . .

"Mommy, what are Gypsies? Communists? Homosexuals?"

"Gypsies are people who live in fancy covered wagons and travel around in Europe. Communists are people in Russia who want everyone to be equal. Homosexuals are men who love other men." It still didn't make much sense. Why did it happen to those kids and not to me?

I asked mommy, "How did we escape?"

"Marsha, Canada is a safe country for the Jews. But we must all protect each other. We must never allow discrimination or hatred against people because of their skin colour or religion." What was discrimination? No one ever talked about this stuff at Queen Elizabeth.

I didn't know any kids in my class. Most of the class never talked to me. Jimmy who sat in the desk behind me would poke me with his pencil. In P.E. team captains never picked me for their volleyball team because I was so small and would gasp from asthma. I would be left squirming and looking at the gym floor while all the other kids were picked until finally the gym teacher said, "Oh Marsha, just go to the red team." Asthma and allergies were a big problem. I had to miss a lot of P.E., but some days I could breathe and run. Today it wasn't so bad.

Joan came up to me at recess. "D'yuh wanna learn to steal?" she asked.

"What's that?"

"Yuh take candy free."

"Okay," I said.

"Yuh got any money?" she asked. I wiped my nose. Mommy had rubbed it with Vaseline, and it didn't feel so rough and sore today. I reached into my sweater pocket. Dry Kleenexes. Good, lots of dry ones and some soggy ones. I dug around in the bottom of my stretched-out sweater pocket and felt two coins.

"I've got two cents," I said.

"Okay, meet me after school."

The bell rang and all the kids ran to line up by grades. As they marched up to the big doors, I was skipping on the gravel and down the hall to her classroom. Joan was one of the biggest girls in Grade 2. Sometimes Joan was a team captain. She wore a white blouse, and on her green sweater she had a peacock pin. The peacock had sparkly coloured stones at the ends of his feathers. Joan had never noticed me before. I looked up at Joan. She had long shiny blonde hair. I wanted to touch it.

I felt in my pocket for the two pennies. Candy, free candy! Jawbreakers three for a penny, peppermint sticks one cent each, white candy cigarettes with red tips, penny toffee suckers, Tootsie Rolls, Double Bubble gum with cartoons in the wrapping paper, Jersey milk chocolate squares in white wrapping with gold letters, little cellophane rolls of sweet pills all different colours. The corner store was right across from the school.

"Wait till a bunch of other kids go in," Joan said. The store was dusty and as soon as I got inside, I started sneezing. "Stop that. Be quiet." I wiped my nose on a crumply but dry Kleenex and tried not to sneeze. In front of us a gang of older kids was looking into the candy bins. Joan waited until some kids went up to the counter. "He's not looking now. Turn around. Stand with your back to the bin so he can't see. Grab some candy and stick it in your pocket." I twisted my hand back and reached into the bin. I felt the cool smooth round jawbreakers, grabbed them tight and pushed them deep into my pocket under the damp Kleenexes. "Okay turn around. Look in the bins and pick something to buy," she whispered.

I stared into the bins at the chocolate squares, two cents each. Did the grocery man know I stole the jawbreakers? Would he grab me and look in my pocket? With damp hands, I picked up two licorice pipes, one cent each, and took them up to the wooden counter. I handed the man my two cents. He took the pennies and rang up the cash register. Then he looked at the next kids behind me. I ran out the door of the store and around the corner into the lane. Was the grocery man following us?

"What'd y'get?" said Joan. I pulled out my five jawbreakers and two licorice pipes. It was a lot of candy for just two cents. But I wished I'd got a Jersey milk chocolate square. Joan snatched all the candy.

"Hey y'got t'share," I said. "What'd y'get?" Joan showed her three peppermint sticks. "Y'got t'share," I said again.

"Okay put out your hand." Joan put one jawbreaker, one licorice pipe, and one peppermint stick into my damp hand.

"Not fair," I said. Joan gave me one more jawbreaker.

"Now y'know how to steal," she said. Joan never spoke to me again.

Trudging home, sucking my sticky peppermint stick, I stopped and turned around looking for the grocery store man. Would he come after me and grab my arm? He used to smile at me. I shouldn't have stolen candy from him. I found some soggy torn Kleenex and wiped my sore dripping nose. Would he tell the principal? Would I get the strap?

Ne T'en Fais Pas [Do Not Worry]

Farren Gillaspie

"Ecoutez! Attentivement! J'ai dit silence!" The nuns swished up and down the aisles, with somber faces, rulers in their hands.

There were morning prayers and a small bottle of milk at lunch to go along with my very sad sandwiches. At times, I thought Mom's lunches were a way of punishing me for leaving her alone when I went to school. She didn't believe in prepping me for school by teaching me to write my name or learn the alphabet. She said that's what the teachers were for. At school, I felt like I was a sponge soaking up all the reading and writing exercises. I was so excited to start printing and learning to read about Dick, Jane, and Spot. I was always getting stars.

Then Mom and Dad separated. Mom and I moved in with an aunt in the country. I thought I had been quite brilliant in kindergarten and was generally well liked by my classmates. Things were different at my new school. This one was an old, one-room schoolhouse. It was heated by a huge pot-bellied stove in the corner, its black stove pipe rising up and disappearing through the roof. There were telltale scorches at the ceiling, evidence of multiple times the pipe had caught fire, the results of an over-zealous fire maker. When I was there, the fire maker and keeper was Eddie. He was the oldest student, just a year younger than the teacher. The desks were ancient. The flip tops were carved with hearts and initials, and stained with ink. Actual ink wells were reserved for Grade 5 and up. The seats were worn smooth by the restless bottoms of several generations. A large portrait of a young Queen Elizabeth hung on the front wall above the teacher's desk. The lingering smell of wood smoke was infused into every crevice in that room.

My mom was adamant that I make a good impression by always being at school on time. She had me start out way earlier than necessary. "Maman, pourquoi m'envoies-tu à l'école de si bonne heure?"

"Ne t'en fais pas," she would say. So, there was lots of time to let my mind wander along the way. I had to walk about a mile along a gravel country road to get there. I was often distracted by birds, squirrels, and foxes. Sometimes I would bend down, pick up a small rock and try to hit a fence post. On one very cold, crisp day with the snow-covered gravel crackling under my feet, I was so distracted by the newness of everything, I froze my ears. No sympathy from my mom. I was supposed to pull my toque with its horrible pom-pom down over my ears.

All grades were in the same room, so we were exposed to all levels of learning. I didn't seem to pick any of it up. My young mind just thought, "Oh well." The teacher was Miss Rose (was that her last name or first? I don't really remember). Since I left home so early, I was always the first one to arrive at school. The room was stifling hot with the first fire of the day. Miss Rose and Eddie would be cheerfully chatting and laughing when I came through the door. Then they would go silent, and I felt like they resented my presence. Miss Rose would be nervously rearranging her notes and pencils. I would mirror her by quietly slipping into my desk, pulling my pencil box out of my messenger bag, which also held my lunch for that day. Mom's lunches hadn't really improved. The messenger bag was a washed burlap bag, simply cut and stitched, with a shoulder strap and a flap. It would be cool today, but back then, not so much.

I seemed to be ignored on the playground, and again I didn't really question it. I was happier on my own anyway. When the students started staring and pointing at me, I just withdrew. In the class, it was Miss Rose's custom to move from one row to another as she checked our work. After lunch she would read a story from a book. We were allowed to put our heads down and rest. I usually drifted off to sleep.

When we had printing assignments, I would just jot down the letters of what I wanted to write, feeling proud that I was so fast. Miss Rose would walk down the aisles and place a star on our work. There were three levels, three colours of stars—gold for 'the best', blue for 'a very good try', and green for 'needs work'. The first time around, I got a green, and I was quite shocked. Following that, she seldom checked my work at all. When she did, I would often excuse myself to go to the outhouse and cry.

It was a nasty January and February. Because of our move, I had started at this school in January. All of the other children had bonded already so that didn't help my situation. The months slowly crawled along, and finally the end of school came in June. My mom and dad reconciled, and we moved into an old house next to my dad's parents. They were English-speaking Baptists. My grandmother took me under her wing.

The school I was to attend that fall was a brand-new school. I was a bit intimidated, but even at six years old, I felt it was a chance to start again, a situation I would experience several times in my life. However, I always felt like a slow learner, that I was 'less than'. I was in my twenties in the middle of a self-help workshop when I realized I am not a slow learner. I had gone from a French Roman Catholic kindergarten, living with my French-speaking mom and grandparents to a totally English-speaking, Protestant school. No one had thought to tell me I had been speaking French and was entering an English school.

A Failure of Democracy
Ellen Woodsworth

I enjoyed moving into the second-floor classroom for Grade 7. The new teacher, Mr. Muller, was handsome, intelligent, and knowledgeable. I was happy that we finally had a social studies class. He began teaching us about world affairs and democracy. Kennedy was the U.S. President. We were young, innocent, and excited.

Mr. Muller wanted to show us democracy in action. He believed that democracy had to be practiced and that young people wanted to learn how. Here was this tall, dark-haired, supportive teacher suggesting that we could be part of democracy. I felt really alive and believed I finally had a teacher who understood me. He suggested, after a discussion with all of us, that the class choose a real situation of concern to us and hold a mock trial. There would be a lawyer for each side with the rest of the students acting as a jury. The class had a difficult time choosing an example. This was the first time most of them had even thought about having any social power in society or had the chance to talk about democracy in practice. In my family, though, discussions about democracy and social justice were the first course.

To my horror, the class finally came up with the idea of putting one of our fellow students, Susan, on trial for being dirty, late, and disheveled. Why didn't Mr. Muller stop the process at that moment and change the topic? For some reason, he was not able to address the emotional momentum to have them reflect thoughtfully on an appropriate, broad, social issue. Susan was probably being tried for always being unhappy, though that wasn't the charge. Why was she being picked on? I was really upset, almost frozen, and afraid. She was a friend of mine but not close. I wonder how close she was to anyone. She seemed to have only one friend. We both lived on the east side of Swansea and were part of a gang of girls who, for one reason or another, all seemed like outsiders, so we played together and occasionally shared birthdays.

The class had to figure out who would defend the accused, Susan, but no one was volunteering. I was really scared at the hostile feelings building and nasty things being said. Though I was shaking, I felt I had to stand up and offer to defend her because the whole situation was so unjust and undemocratic. My dad was a lawyer, so I had some vague ideas of what to do, and Susan was a friend. The whole thing was so awful, unfair, and vicious. I had to stand up and protect her against the attacks. It was a horrifying example of democracy not working for the poorest and most vulnerable. The idea was frightening, that a whole class could attack the most vulnerable student in the name of democracy.

Susan was forced to stand up at the front of the room. I stood beside her. We could feel our terror building as the students lashed out. I attempted to defend her while feeling the whole situation was becoming dangerous, but I didn't know how to stop a class of 13-year-olds. The teacher, the only one with power in the situation, didn't stop it. The students were being allowed to call out nasty, personal comments about her misery. They were standing up and shouting at us, almost climbing out of their chairs to attack. Mr. Muller should have stopped the whole thing and made us realize that this was not democracy but a crowd lynching. He could have used it to describe what was happening to the Blacks in the southern United States.

At the end of the mock trial, Susan was found guilty as charged by the class. I just felt helpless, and we both felt so vulnerable and terrified. I kept thinking: Why didn't Mr. Muller stop it at any point? He was allowing raging teenage anger to be taken out on Susan, exploding the very notion of fairness that he was trying to show us. The Grade 7 class, which had become a mob, decided the punishment. The class was to go downstairs to the cavernous basement gym, line up in a long row with their legs spread and Susan would have to crawl through their legs as they hit her.

The class was really excited at their power, like animals moving in for the kill. I felt paralyzed as we were forced out of the classroom by the pouring mass, down the two flights of stairs, and into the gym. Why didn't anyone stop us when they heard the crowd pounding down the stairs in the midst of class time? I can hardly write this true story as my hand is shaking so much fifty-seven years later. The students created a long line, and Susan was forced to crawl through them as they beat her. All of a sudden, she stood up and ran out of the gym. I looked around shocked and then ran after her. The students were outraged and began shouting at us, and then started after us as we ran for our lives.

I ran up the stairs but I couldn't find Susan. At first, I was wandering around the empty hallways where a teacher stopped me to ask what I was doing, but it didn't feel safe to tell her. I finally figured out Susan must be in the Special Education classroom on the main floor where she would have known the teacher was supportive as she used to go to classes with her. I found her there. We were safe for the moment. However, neither the teacher nor either of us knew what to do. We were so shaken and afraid that the school itself had become dangerous. We couldn't go back to the classroom, and the kids were probably outside for recess, so we couldn't go to the playground.

I finally got up my courage and decided to walk down the long hall to the principal's office and call my mother. The secretary wanted to know what was happening because I was shaking and my voice was trembling. I must have looked upset but I still didn't trust anyone at that point. I knew that the students had formed a mob and were looking for us. Thankfully, the secretary let me use the phone. I wonder why no one told the principal? Why wasn't the mob being stopped?

Luckily my mom was working at home that day and once she could get me to calm down enough to tell her what was happening, agreed to come and get us. She could tell that I was really afraid.

She agreed to drive over and meet us at the door of the auditorium, which we thought would be safe as it was away from the playground. We figured that the kids wouldn't look for us there. About the time we thought my mom would drive up, we walked quietly down the hall hoping no one would see us. There was the mob. They were gathering outside the doors. We had nowhere else to go. Terrified, we opened the doors, then dashed through the screaming gang to Mom's small VW and piled in while they were yelling and hitting us. They thumped the car as my mom revved up and sped away from the school.

There was a dead silence in the car. We gradually began to feel safe but were in shock and really upset. My mom asked us to tell her what had happened. Susan was silent. We were so shaken. I tried to explain what seemed really complicated to me, and she didn't seem to understand how it could have occurred. It took Mom ten minutes or less to get to the top of our street where it met Susan's street, and then she stopped. Much to my horror, Mom asked Susan to walk home from there. I just figured Mom would drive her home. It was at least four long blocks away, and we were both still really terrified that somehow the students would reappear. Susan was feeling awful, and now Mom was abandoning her. Why wouldn't Mom just drive her home? I had stood up to the students' abuse based on the values she and my dad had taught me. She was probably mad at me for dragging her into the mess, away from the work she was doing, but she was a social worker!

I still don't know why she dropped Susan off at the top of the long hill home. I had tried to explain the whole situation as she drove, but I don't remember her saying much. Looking back now, I wonder if my mom might have been afraid herself, remembering the nasty mob mentality that had attacked her politically and then removed her from her elected position as president of the local PTA when she signed the Stockholm Peace Petition. That gang would have been the parents of those kids who were attacking us. At that moment, I felt totally betrayed by my mom.

I have always wondered what happened to Susan. I wonder if she was being abused at home to be so unhappy. Mr. Muller got into trouble, and our class got a talking-to. Susan was forced to come back to class. There was a deep silence, and no one talked about it again. I felt awful that I hadn't been able to protect her from the mob, and to this day I am still afraid of mobs.

Mr. Muller had wanted to show us how democracy could work in the classroom, but the model he created for us had turned into a witch-hunt. He failed to teach us that democracy is supposed to protect the rights of the individual.

My Early Years in School
Greta Hurst

My kindergarten picture hangs in the hall, and I sometimes pause to look at it. I'm standing in the back row in a sailor-type blouse which was part of the uniform the girls wore. Miss Baisley, our teacher, is standing in front of a Christmas tree, with the boys on one side and the girls on the other. Some Nativity scenes are on the wall behind us. It's just before Christmas, 1941.

In 1939, when I was three and my sister was twelve months old, our parents heard 'good news' about the German economy. A German neighbour had told them that Germany was booming, and everyone had a job—it might be the time for my father to return to his native land. My parents sold everything, except for personal belongings, and booked passage on a ship going to Hamburg. They had given up their flat and were ready to board the ship in Montreal's harbour. Apparently, they hadn't been listening to the radio because, at that very moment, Hitler had declared war. Fortunately, they hadn't yet boarded the ship. Neither of them had Canadian citizenship, and since the ship was regarded as German, if they had boarded, my father would have been forced to return to Germany directly. Mother, my sister, and I could have gone to Germany as well, or, because she was Norwegian, the three of us could have gone to Norway. Instead, we stayed in Montreal, and my parents tried to make do.

My kindergarten was in the center of Montreal, and pupils came from all parts of the city. Miss Baisley was a very kind teacher, aware that many students were in a large group for the first time. I was overwhelmed by the number of children in my class and was too shy to make any friends. My mother told Miss Baisley in confidence that my father wasn't Norwegian, as she generally claimed, but

German. She must have done this to get Miss Baisley to keep an eye out for me. It was the third year of World War II. On the east coast of Canada, people were terrified of a German invasion. A German submarine had been spotted in the St. Lawrence River although it was never verified. German people in Canada were lucky compared to Japanese Canadians, who had their properties and businesses confiscated. We heard they were relocated to Alberta. Canadian authorities wanted us to believe they were spies for Japan. Nothing like that happened to people of German descent living here, but I was too young to realize that we also were regarded with suspicion.

I have little memory of what I did that year in kindergarten, but I do remember there were some large dolls that I admired though never had the chance to hold. One day, I asked Miss Baisley if I could hold a doll, and she persuaded the little girl who always got to hold them to hand me one of the dolls. For a shy person like me, it was a bit of joy I would always remember.

My first-grade teacher was Miss Ford. She turned out to be very nasty to me. It seems I had lost my shyness and was now a talker. One day, she obviously had enough of my chatter with my neighbour and decided to make an example of me. We had a cloak room attached to our class where we hung our coats and left our boots. Winters are very harsh in Montreal so the cloak room was always full. Miss Ford spanked me in the cloak room where no one could see her doing that. She then marched me to the basket beside her desk and put me in, bum first, and opened the classroom door, so everyone passing could see me in my shame. Mother was furious when she heard what happened. The next day Mother came to school to see Miss Ford and berated her for the punishment she had inflicted on me. I was thoroughly shamed by both the incident and my mother's loud anger in berating Miss Ford. Happily, neither Miss Ford nor my mother shamed me again.

Miss Toy, my second-grade teacher, was different. She was the first Japanese person I had ever met. It was surprising to see her in Montreal as I thought all Japanese people lived in Alberta. She was small in stature, timid, and totally different from my previous teachers. I felt sorry for her—her terror was so evident. I don't remember much about that year, but I knew I'd never be punished.

Miss Forster, my third-grade teacher, had apparently heard in the teachers' room that my father was German. The father of one boy in our class was a pilot in the air force and had been shot down, which the boy had just found out the day before. When Miss Forster expressed her sympathy to the boy, every one turned and stared at me in anger. It took me a long time to figure out that Miss Baisley must have told the other teachers about my father. She may have tried to engage the other teachers to be kind to me, but that didn't happen. In fact, Miss Forster had decided to 'out' me by staring at me. I'm not sure how the students could have known, and I never found out.

The good news that year was that I got my first friend, Pearl. She didn't live with her parents but with an aunt who ran a boarding house. They had a Chinese cook, which I thought amazing. She and I were definitely the odd ducks in the room. Pearl gave me a picture of herself in a tank top, proudly rowing a boat, and I was so impressed. I was very sad because after third grade, I never saw Pearl again. The next year we had to transfer to another school.

I transferred to Aberdeen School on St. Denis Street which was only a few blocks away from where we lived. St. Denis Street divided the Anglophones on the west side of the street from the Francophones on the east side. It was in a working-class section of Montreal, and the students didn't wear uniforms in public schools. Although Mother was concerned I might be beaten up, fortunately that didn't happen. The good news was that there was a candy store just across the street. As we weren't allowed to eat candy, I took the rare opportunity to steal change from Mother's purse to indulge my sweet tooth. Aberdeen was totally different from my previous school. Although I was still timid, and afraid I might get picked on, the other children just ignored me.

The next year, Mother took my sister and me to her birth place in Norway for four months. Experiencing a different country, one that had lived through occupation during the war, allowed me a new perspective on life. I returned to Canada knowing in my heart that things would be better.

Death Equals Silence
Chris Morrissey

One Monday morning in mid-September, I went into my fourth-grade class at Sacred Heart School in Prince George. Sister Mary was sitting at her desk waiting for us to settle down. Once we were all sitting still, she stood up in front of the class. She stood very straight, emphasized by the long black habit she wore. She looked very serious. We all sat very still.

"Class, I have very sad news today. On Saturday, Pamela, your classmate, drowned in Salmon River. She was swimming in the river, and she wasn't strong enough for the current. Her dad jumped in to try and save her, but he didn't reach her in time. The RCMP are looking for her body." Nobody moved. We could hear the clock on the wall ticking.

After a few minutes, Sister said, "It is very sad but now we have to get back to work. We were working on our decimals and learning to add and subtract them. Open your exercise books and copy the examples from the blackboard. I'll give you half an hour to work on them quietly." Next you could hear pages turning, pencils scratching.

Finally, the day was over. As soon as I got home, I told my mother, "Pamela from my class drowned in Salmon River on Saturday." My mom was dressed in a pair of blue slacks, a pink flowery blouse all protected by an apron that had been embroidered with flowers. She was standing in the kitchen in front of the sink peeling potatoes, carrots, and turnips. The pressure cooker was next to her.

"Yes, very sad. I heard it on the news this morning. Do you have homework to do? Go and change out of your uniform, then begin your homework before Daddy gets home for supper."

The next Tuesday when we arrived at school and were all in our places, Sister Mary said, "In a few minutes we'll be going over to the church for Pamela's funeral." The church was right next to the school. We were all quiet. "Line up now. When we get to the church, I'll lead you to the benches where we will be sitting."

The coffin was carried in and placed in the middle aisle in front of the altar and next to the bench where her mother, father, and brother were sitting. Mass began. The priest, dressed in the usual robes, approached the coffin swinging the thurible with incense. Suddenly, the mother began to howl very loudly. It seemed to go on and on. I had never heard anything like it before. My body went stiff. I could hear my breathing. I thought I might wet my pants. Somehow, I got through the Mass. We waited in our places until the coffin, the family, and most of the people had left the church. Then it was our turn to file out silently. We went back to school and back to work.

When I arrived home at the end of the day, I changed out of my school uniform and went to do my homework as usual. Dad came home from work and after some brief greetings, he sat in his armchair and opened his newspaper.

"We went to Pamela's funeral today."

"That's good, Christine." He went back to reading his paper.

Time for bed. How will I get into bed in the dark? The light switch was next to the door and my bed was in the corner. What about the things under the bed? Will they grab my legs as I try to get into bed? Can I run fast enough? Gritting my teeth, I switched off the light, ran and jumped on to the bed.

———◇———

Years passed. There were no other funerals I had to attend. My next encounter with death was after I entered the convent. During one of our instructions, the Postulant Mistress said, "Once a month, we have 'Recollection Sunday'. Instead of our regular meditation on the day's gospel, what we do is meditate on death. This coming Sunday, this is what we will be doing." In silence, we gathered in the chapel and took our places. One of the sisters began to read from the customs book.

"One day we all will die. We will not know the day nor the hour." Somewhere buried in my memory are such words as "being eaten by worms." As a 17-year-old, it almost scared me to death! This was part of my life every month for the next few years. I often fell asleep. It was the only way I could avoid facing my childhood fears.

In the early 1970s, the Catholic Church began a period of renewal. Religious communities of women also began to change. For many years, we had lived very structured lives. For those of us that had begun this life as young women, our emotional and communication lives had been stunted. There were many adult skills that we had not learned: making decisions about anything, social conversation, and finances. To help us adapt to the changes, the Superior hired Suzanne to meet with us once a month. She provided us with topics for discussion, and part way through the day, she would send us off in pairs. Every month, Catriona asked me to be her partner. She said to me once, "I like discussing with you because you often say what I'm thinking."

Catriona's parents were celebrating their 'Golden Jubilee.' She was given permission to go back to Ireland for three weeks to participate in the celebration. She was gone for about a week, when at supper the Superior shared the news that Catriona's mother had died of a stroke. Two weeks later, we received word that her father had died of a heart attack when he was on his way to the lawyer's office to make his will.

Suddenly, I began to shake, my mouth went dry, and my breathing became laboured. I knew that the custom was to send a 'holy card' and to write letters of condolence. I sat at the desk. Hand shaking. Thoughts buzzing around like bees in a field full of flowers. What can I write? I don't know what to say. I'll do it tomorrow. But I didn't.

Catriona returned from Ireland. We both continued on with our day-to-day work in our respective cities. A couple of months later, I was working on putting together a visual story of what our lives were like at different ages and stages as a tool to use in presentations to attract other young women to join us. I asked Catriona if she would participate. I made an appointment and drove to the city she was living in. We sat down with tape recorder and camera.

"Can you share with us what it is that brought you to religious life and why you have stayed." Silence. No answer.

She lifted her head, looked at me and said, "I can't do this." Then she asked, "Why didn't you write to me?"

"I just didn't know what to write," I said. Silence. Breathing. "How are you doing?" She began to cry.

So began her healing, and mine.

Forty years later I held her hand as she took her last breaths.

A More Masculine Pursuit
Don Martin

"All you ever do is hang out with girls," Steve Zillah said to me. "It's unnatural."

One of the playground bullies had just shoved me to the ground and mocked me in falsetto. After the tough guy trotted off laughing, I got up, brushed myself off, and asked Steve why other boys are always so mean. Steve was my neighbour and one of the few males in my fourth-grade class that I trusted. He was a freckled, gangly kid who smelled like fried ham. He got bullied, too, for his nerdy intelligence, but he was a lot more athletic and had plenty of friends among the other boys.

"We have to find you a more masculine pursuit," Steve said. "You should be more like one of the guys. Why don't you learn a sport, like baseball? You could start out easy, you know, collect baseball cards. Follow a player you like. Learn the rules." I raised my eyebrows skeptically. "It's worth a try," he said. And so Steve Zillah and I spent the summer before fifth grade honing my skills at baseball.

My dad had coached a baseball team when he was a younger man. I think he was secretly thrilled (and relieved) I was showing an interest in the game. He gave me pointers and bought me a variety of equipment, including a top-of-the-line mitt that was oh-so-crucial to fifth-grade status. It bore the signature of Roberto Clemente, Jr. who was in the World Series the year before. He was a hero in my largely Latino community, though I think he signed as 'Bob' above the engraved lettering of his full name to appeal to a broader audience. For a white kid like me, his wasn't the 'best' name you could get, but still, it was a really cool outfielder's mitt, and I lovingly worked the stiffness out of its tawny leather.

My family had a small farm with a big pasture near Yakima in arid eastern Washington. That summer, I spent hours in the field tossing a ball in the air and swatting at it, perfecting my power hit. I painted a target on a piece of plywood, propped it against some bales of hay, and worked on my pitching speed and accuracy. Steve and the Peterson boys from across the street came over almost every afternoon to play 'work up'. Whenever I got a spare nickel, I'd bike to the corner grocery store for a pack of gum with a trading card inside. Steve and I collected all the top players, and I tried to memorize the stats on each athlete.

I was ready as I could be.

It was 1961, a year of hope and change. We had a new, inspiring, young president. We sent a man into space. We lined up to get the newest polio vaccine served on sugar cubes. I was sure it would be a good year. School had been in session for three weeks, but it still felt like summer. The chilly nights were turning the apples red and making autumn palpable with the smell of over-ripe foliage and a sense of changing sunlight. Daytime temperatures were still in the eighties as we settled in to our lessons at Wide Hollow School. Steve snuck a transistor radio in his pocket, so we could listen in to news of the World Series whenever we had chance. The Reds vs. the Yanks—an easy allusion for Cold War headline writers. Roger Maris had just beat out Mickey Mantle to take away Babe Ruth's single-season home run record. I was already impressing some of the guys with my ability to recite batting averages.

My school, Wide Hollow, was built in the 1930s, surrounded by apple orchards. It was a classic, two-story brick structure with an arched entrance and classrooms or offices on either side of a wide central hallway. Teachers had to use long transom poles to open the tops of the ten-foot windows. At the main doorway was a hefty wooden stairway worn smooth by the feet of generations of farm kids. Ground floor classrooms housed grades one to four. Upstairs had grades five to eight. This was my first year on the top floor, and as someone who was short for my age, I desperately wanted to be seen as one of the big kids.

Most of the time we used the main stairs, but on each end of the building there were narrower staircases. To get to the playground's baseball diamond, we took the stairs on the west end of the building. This was also the section where, on the second floor, the eighth graders had their classrooms. They weren't that much older than us, but puberty made them seem like adults.

The playground at Wide Hollow was huge, maybe ten acres. So much space was great for a kid like me. I was usually able to find a safe spot. My closest friends were always girls. At recess the girls and I would run to the farthest corner of the playground to be away from the boys and their mean, oafish ways. We would talk about movies and books and TV shows, about teen idols, the latest fashions, and which 45s we wanted to buy. Sometimes we'd fold squares of paper into 'fortune tellers' with answers hidden under a flap, and take turns lifting them to reveal secrets about love and marriage. Though I was resolved to shed my former image and be more like one of the guys, after less than a month I already missed hanging out with my female friends.

For those first few days in September, I was content to sit on the sidelines of the baseball diamond and watch the older boys play. Eventually Steve got me to do warm-ups with him along the third base line, demonstrating our throwing and grounding skills in hopes of being noticed. I don't think anyone was impressed. The guy who had teased me last year yelled, "Hey Martin, go play with the girls." Steve told me to shrug it off.

The eighth graders were required to let some of the younger kids into their noontime games. The best and most popular were picked first, of course, so it was quite a while before I got in. I was filled with anxiety when I finally heard, "Martin, you're up." I instinctively knew this was the moment on which my baseball career at Wide Hollow would depend. At the plate, I took a firm grip and the butchest stance I could for someone under five feet. Duane Prosser's older brother was pitching. He was one of the school's top athletes. Duane and I were classmates and pretty good friends. Maybe his brother would go easy on me.

My dad told me never to swing at the first pitch and I didn't. Good thing. It was intentionally high and wide. Ball one. I took a breath and concentrated. The next one was low, but I went for it anyway and missed. The catcalls started. I tried to calm myself, tapped my bat on the plate, and spit. Fortunately I got another ball. The fourth pitch zinged across the plate and I whiffed again. Strike two. Now the badgering was in falsetto, "You swing like your girlfriends." I was face to face with a future of humiliation. As the next pitch screamed toward the plate, I closed my eyes and swung as hard as I could. To my astonishment, I felt it connect, and when I looked, I saw the ball arching into the far corner of the playground where I had always tried to escape. A home run.

I got a grudging bit of admiration from the other players. The guy with the falsetto yelled, "Way to keep your eye on the ball, Martin." Steve and Duane were hooting as I rounded third. I had survived for now.

After a while the bell rang and all the guys who had been playing hard in the hot sun crowded into the narrow staircase at the end of the building. Some genuinely warm back slaps and butt pats. The jostling of muscular upperclassmen. The dizzying aroma of boys who were becoming men. Something was awakening inside me, but I didn't have the words yet to understand it.

The glory of my home run moment, however, evaporated like dew in the desert. Baseball had done little to change my status, and my fascination faded by the end of the season. Girls, I decided, were far more interesting and intelligent. Except for maybe Steve.

Library Day
River Glen

The fourth-grade class walked quickly down the mint-green hall with its darker and lighter green patterned, polished, linoleum-tile floors. The kids were reasonably quiet as they moved two-by-two past the fifth and sixth-grade classrooms toward their destination, the school library. As she went by the open doorways, Julie glanced into each room, interested in what the bigger kids were learning, but, in the stream of classmates, she was forced to keep up and keep moving.

From the cool, subdued light of the hall, she turned into the library doorway and entered a sun-filled room. There were light oak tables and chairs. The oak card catalog with its banks of drawers looked very business-like. In between the tall bookshelves were a few bulletin boards with cheerful coloured pictures and titles of the current recommended books. By the desk where the librarian sat, and where you checked out the books, was a circle of little chairs that the first and second graders would sit on for their story time. It seemed to Julie like a long time since she had been that small.

The teacher, Miss Travis, stage-whispered that everyone must lower their voices and sit down at the tables. Julie sat across from her best friend. The librarian, Mrs. Roberts, with her light grey, permed hair, came over and began showing several books she thought the class would enjoy. When she finished, she gave the class permission to get up and go look for a book.

Julie went immediately to the low shelf at the far end of the fiction section where authors with the letter 'W' were kept. She felt happiness wash over her, seeing the several books by the author she loved, Laura Ingalls Wilder, lined up in sequential order. Her hand reached down carefully. She removed the third volume, which she clutched protectively to her chest as she carried it back to the table. With the excitement of anticipation, she opened the book and saw the illustrations and words which were like dear friends. She had been reading these books over and over again since the year before when her third-grade teacher had read them aloud to the class every day after lunch. Julie had fallen deeply in love with them with no room in her heart for any others.

Then Miss Travis walked over to her carrying a book.

"Julie, I want you to take a look at this book. It is like the Little House books. I know you will like it."

Julie tightened her fingers around her Plum Creek copy. The teacher was looking down at her with sympathetic eyes, but her smile was drawing down into a determined straight line. Julie understood the power Miss Travis had in that moment and only wanted to grab her book and flee with it to safety.

"That's a good girl," Miss Travis said, as she slid her book toward Julie with one hand and took hold of Julie's book with the other. Julie resisted only as long as it took for the look on her teacher's face to become less patient. The exchange had been made. Julie sat starring at the usurper through tear-filled eyes. Miss Travis was already at another table, bending over another of her twenty-eight pupils, pointing to a page in their book. She smiled warmly again at Julie from the distance.

Reluctantly, Julie opened the new book and turned the pages, mechanically at first, barely even seeing the words. But a funny thing happened in not a very long period of time—the story caught her attention. By the time library hour was over, Julie had read a couple of chapters, and Miss Travis came over with another book by the same author.

"You check these out for this week and let me know how you like them."

"Can I take my favourite out also?" Julie asked with some pleading in her voice.

"Yes, but make sure you read the new ones first," Miss Travis replied in a firmer voice. And Julie did.

From then on, new books came very easily, but even in eighth grade Julie still read her favourites. Her home life was chaotic, and the world of her favourite author was the world in which she felt most safe.

Mickey and the Martian
Farren Gillaspie

I must have been about thirteen, and I had gone through seven years of bullying at school. I was one of about four or five boys who were constantly bullied, not because we were gay, but because we were farmers' sons. Busing in from the farm meant that we couldn't stay after school to play sports with our classmates. We had chores even on the weekends. So even if there was a remote chance that we might bond, the opportunity never presented itself.

My self-image was extremely poor. I felt that my forehead was too large, my hairline was too high, it looked like I had a receding hairline. My knees were knobby. I was skinny and had that haunting, dark look around my eyes. Nothing seemed right with me. To add to that, in the midst of my despair, I would often think, my hair will fall out, my teeth will fall out, my fingernails and toenails will grow long, and the cuticles grow over because I just won't be able to keep up with the maintenance. A glimmer of hope came when I saw a television show called *My Favorite Martian*, and I thought, "That's me. I'm an alien. Uncle Martin, (the Martian, Ray Walston) was probably my real Dad."

Mom was adamant that just because I lived on a farm, I didn't need to look like I lived on a farm. She refused to let me wear jeans and t-shirts. Ironically, the village boys dressed like farmers, not only wearing jeans and t-shirts but in the spring wearing rubber boots! I didn't even dare approach Mom with that idea. My clothes, in fact, usually consisted of casual slacks with jersey knit shirts in the spring, or patterned shirts with cardigans in the winter. My shoes were sensible lace-up ones with thick soles that I could not possibly wear out. Everything was ordered from the Eaton's mail order catalogue. It would be nice to think I might have been a trend setter, but no, I was a true geek, even though I had never heard of the word. Maybe I was the first real geek?

My main tormentor all through public school was Mickey Hunter. Where I was blond, blue-eyed, skinny, and introverted, he was a very handsome dark-haired, brown-eyed boy with a beautiful dark complexion that glowed. He was outgoing, and everyone gravitated toward him. He was the first one I noticed in my Grade 1 class. I thought we would be best friends. That lasted about half a day.

Mickey was very academically skilled as well. Meanwhile, I had gotten off to a slow start because my parents had no idea how to prepare me for school. Mom said I didn't need to learn my letters or numbers at home. That was what I was going to school for. To make matters worse, until the previous year I had lived with my French grandparents, and I hardly spoke English.

Mickey taunted me about everything, from my clothes to my lack of athletic skills, and my school grades. First term I was close to failing. Mickey, of course, was the top of our class. There wasn't much I could do about a lot of things, but I realized, in my quiet way, that if I could be the top of the class that would help me get back at him. By the end of the year, I was third highest in my class. The following years through public school, Mickey and I were neck-to-neck as far as our grades went. When he got a paper back that was higher than mine, he would gloat and wave it at me. When I got a higher mark, I would think, "I am a Martian. I am wiser and better," and I would just smile like Uncle Martin would. It drove Mickey quite mad.

As an adult, I always wondered why Mickey had been so mean and focused on me. I had never realized that maybe he was jealous of me. Maybe he wanted to be a blond, blue-eyed boy. Unfortunately, I will never know. Mickey was an early bloomer. I saw a photo of him in his thirties. His trim waist line was gone, and he was quite portly. Last year, I heard from a friend that Mickey had died of a heart attack. He was fifty-six.

Unintended Consequences
Janie Cawley

I hated typing class. I mean I *really* hated it. The teacher, Mr. Dawes, had a military approach. Before the bell rang to start the class, we all had to be seated in front of our typewriters. He would then shout, "Remove covers!" We would place the covers with precision behind the typewriters. He would then shout, "Fingers on home row!" Next command was, "Correct posture!" He would pause here to correct any hands resting on a keyboard, shoulders slumping, feet not properly resting on the floor, and then, finally, he would start the drills.

The first drill was to sequentially hit the letters of the home row 'asdf' with the left hand and ';lkj' with the right. We repeated this drill twenty times. We moved on. "Around and round the rugged rock, the ragged rascal ran." This too was repeated twenty times. To relieve the boredom, I once tried typing the sentence backwards. This, however, slowed my typing down so much that I drew Mr. Dawes' attention. Not a desirable thing. Our next drill was to type sentences that were on the blackboard. The last drill was to type one or two business letters dictated by Mr. Dawes. All these drills, including the reading of paragraphs, were interspersed with shouts of, "Eyes up!"

I hated typing class.

Then, an opportunity to insert a little excitement into typing class presented itself. Jack, a friend of mine who I had met in Chemistry Club, told me he couldn't go to a much-anticipated chemistry lecture at the University of British Columbia because he had been grounded, probably for life. Jack was not the kind of kid who would get grounded, especially not for life. I asked him what he had done.

"I wanted to see if I could produce the kind of explosive powder that magicians use when they want to distract or amaze their audience," he said. "It's highly explosive. Touching it sets it off."

"How did you make it?" I asked.

"I put an iodine crystal in a coffee filter and poured ammonia over it. When the coffee filter dried, I collected the white powder on a sheet of paper. I had quite a pile of it," he said proudly.

"What went wrong?" I asked.

Jack sighed. "Dad came into the room without knocking. He rested his hand on my desk—right on top of the powder. It exploded. All of it. I mean it's not like it was really dangerous. All that happened was a huge bang, a lot of smoke and a big purple stain on the paper the powder was on. Dad was furious, Mom was even madder."

"He should have knocked," I commented.

"You can say that again," said Jack.

"So, if he wasn't really hurt, why the grounding?" I asked. Jack looked a little uncomfortable. "Unfortunately, Dad was just home from the hospital, recovering from a heart attack."

"Oh." There wasn't much more I could say. While I was very glad that Jack's father hadn't suffered another heart attack, this was not the first thought that crossed my mind. My first thought was: Wow, wouldn't this powder on the home row of the typing keys be a great way to disrupt Mr. Dawes' class?

I immediately started planning.

Creating the powder wasn't as easy as I had imagined. It *was* highly explosive. Until I perfected a technique of getting the powder off the coffee filter and into the slightly crumpled, letter-sized envelope that I had found in the kitchen junk drawer, there were several misadventures. I had taken my cue from what happened with Jack's father and never tried making any powder unless I was home alone. The misadventures did, however, leave a purple stain on my fingers. I wasn't worried about this being potential evidence of a connection with the disruption of the typing class because, if my plan worked, every student in the typing class would have purple stains on their fingers. My time spent reading mysteries had not, as my mother insisted, been a complete waste of time. I did pick up a lot of information about concealing evidence.

When my mom asked about the stain, I explained it away by muttering something about finger painting experiments in art class. That got quite a snort from my father. I hoped it was an expression of his opinion on art class and not any suspicion that I might, in fact, be doing something else. I had noticed a lingering smell of ammonia in my room after each of my production sessions.

Finally, I thought I had enough powder. Even if I didn't have enough, I was nervous about making any more. Getting the powder to school was a bit of a trial. I carried the powder envelope in my hand as I walked to school. I couldn't think what else to do with it. I didn't want to risk stuffing it in my book bag or in my pocket. About halfway to school, I heard a small crackling sound behind me. I turned my head and saw what looked like tiny electrical sparks going off. The envelope had obviously developed what must have been a very tiny hole, and some of the powder was getting out. As soon as the powder hit the ground, it made a little flash. I very carefully changed the angle at which I was carrying the envelope. The crackling stopped. As far as I could tell, no one paid me the slightest attention.

I stored the envelope of powder in my locker. At lunch break, I nonchalantly took the envelope to the top floor of the school and into the typing room. I had already realized that my plan of putting powder on every home row of every typewriter would have to be abandoned. The inconvenient fact of how easily the powder could be set off made a thorough coverage of the keys impossible. I did, however, manage to get some powder on some home row keys of all the typewriters. There were some purple stains on and around the typewriters. I just hoped nobody would notice.

I had almost made it to the lunch room when the bell went off for afternoon classes. Typing was the first class after lunch. As usual, before the bell finished ringing, we were all seated in front of our typewriters. At Mr. Dawes' command all covers were removed. Then Mr. Dawes shouted, "Fingers on home row!"

This was as far as my planning had gone. I had not given one thought to what would happen when a room full of teenage girls had their typing keys seem to explode beneath their fingers.

Well, it was bedlam. Girls were screaming and running around the classroom. Mr. Dawes shouting only added to the chaos. Someone went out into the hall and pulled the fire alarm. Our school was used to having fire drills once or twice a year. Our typing class was right next to the stairwell, and all the typing students rushed headlong down the stairs. I was at the tail end of the rush. It dawned on me that there were more flaws to my terrific plan than those I had already encountered. What if someone fell, fainted, threw up? I held my breath until all my classmates were safely down the stairs and out on the playing field.

I was happy to see that the rest of the school was evacuating in the brisk and orderly way we had been practicing for the last three years. As none of the teachers were expecting a fire drill, they didn't have their usual clipboards to check off students. Other than that, it would have looked like any other fire drill. However, before the school was quite finished evacuating, the fire department arrived with more equipment than I thought possible. Masks and breathing apparatus, hoses, axes, fire extinguishers. I tried to talk to one of the firefighters, not sure exactly what I was going to say, and thinking that after I talked to him, I would be grounded for life. But he just yelled at me to move on.

Apparently, it didn't take the firefighters long to spot the purple stains on the typing keys and figure out what had happened. I saw the fire chief talking to the principal, who looked furious. The three short rings of the all-clear signal went. Everyone was told to go back to their classes, except for the typing class, which was told to go to the library to complete the hour as a study period. There was no studying done. There were a lot of excited voices saying things like, "What do you think happened? Who could have done such a thing? If they ever catch who did it . . ."

Two hours later, at the end of the school day, after everyone had gathered in homerooms, the principal came on the intercom. He didn't seem to have calmed down from when the fire chief had been talking with him. The principal lectured us on how irresponsible this outrageous prank had been, how the student responsible had endangered lives, what if someone had fallen down the stairs while evacuating, and on and on. There was nothing he said that I had not already, if belatedly, thought about. It was clearly my duty to go and confess. Just as I started to lift myself out of my chair, the principal said, "No student will be dismissed until the boy who did this reports to my office."

I sat back down.

True Religion
Cyndia Cole

Now that I'm in the seventh grade and have started junior high school, at church I get to graduate from Sunday School to Christian Youth. For five years, I've earned pins for perfect attendance at Sunday School. I also have a large collection of gold stars for memorizing Bible quotations. When they tell me to read one chapter from the New Testament every night, I do, just like I do all my school assignments.

My family lives on a military base where church is held in a chapel that caters to all faiths. The early service on Sunday has a plain cross and a variety of chaplains who are pastors from all the Protestant denominations. That's when we go. After early service is over, they open the curtains to reveal a crucifix, and the kneeling benches fold down for the Catholic Mass. I'm pretty sure they hold Jewish worship too, but not on Sunday.

Christian Youth is led by the youngest minister and his wife. They're supposed to relate to us well because they're only a few years older than the seniors in twelfth grade. He's slim and has a blond crew cut. He wears normal clothes like chinos and an Oxford shirt, no clerical collar. She's got long straight black hair which makes her look a bit like that new folksinger, Joan Baez.

I'm hanging back in the doorway because I'm the newest and the youngest in the group of twenty-five bubbly teens. The minister starts up a game. He picks Mary to sit on a chair facing the rest of us. Mary is sixteen, and you can tell that she's the kind who's so naïve and shy she's never even been on a date with a boy. The kids don't see her as 'cute' or 'popular'. No one thinks she's 'sexy'.

The minister blindfolds Mary. He and his wife kneel on either side of her chair. Only the minister speaks. He says, "Mary, I'm going to take off your shoe and help you try on some nylon stockings." Mary nods, puzzled but totally trusting. It's actually the minister's wife who takes off Mary's right shoe and puts her hands in a circle pretending to fit a stocking on Mary's bare leg. She slides the circle of her hands up around the ankle to Mary's calf.

The minister says, "How's that? Do they fit?" Mary is pulling her arms in tight to her body and shrinking herself up.

"Okay," she squeezes out tentatively.

"Let's try them up a little higher," the minister says with a bold tease in his voice. His wife's hands move over Mary's knee and around her thigh. The kids watching start to titter. I can see Mary is horrified and looking for a way out but is frozen. "I think we need to pull your stockings up a bit further," the minister smirks.

Mary squirms and blurts out, "No thanks." Her face is bright red. The Christian youth seem to be universally amused, almost on the edge of laughter.

"Just a little higher," taunts the minister as his wife's hands slide around Mary's upper thigh and disappear beneath her full skirt, approaching her crotch. Mary looks like a person being tortured who is powerless to make it stop. Shame rolls off her in waves that reach me all the way at the far end of the room. "Well, okay," says the minister suddenly taking off Mary's blindfold. She sees that it's not his hands but his wife's so close to her private parts. The whole room bursts out in laughter. Mary slinks off to another seat and stares at the floor, looking mortified.

I am oblivious to whatever happens next in Christian Youth group. At the age of twelve, I am so inexperienced that I don't really get the sexual nature of the 'joke'. Maybe part of this is that I would find a woman's hands more sexual than a man's, though just as invasive. But, of course, I don't know this about myself yet and don't have it available to explain the dissonance to me. I am lost in my head, trying to figure out what this game has to do with learning about Jesus and his mercy. I am in agony along with Mary, as though I, too, am the victim. I notice no one speaks to her or makes any gesture to indicate empathy. I am dumbfounded that the minister and his wife, the mouthpieces of Christian love, our exemplars of 'good people', have just humiliated an innocent young woman. And not a single soul intervenes. Instead, everyone participates. I can't answer the questions I keep asking myself: Why do they think torturing a girl is funny? Why is she ashamed and not them? And why doesn't anyone take her part?

Not long after this, I decide I am an Atheist. When I declare this to my mother, she is deeply shocked but knows that she can't make me go to church any more. I have never met a single atheist. I've never encountered anyone who declares themselves to be a person without religion. In the mid-1960s, here in 'middle America', what I've done is unthinkable. Atheists and agnostics exist only in books, like the ones I've read by Bertrand Russell, *Why I Am Not a Christian*, and by Samuel Butler, *The Way of All Flesh*. I decide I'll have to find some people who write books because I know I don't belong with these 'good' people here. Until then, I expect I'll be alone—but at least I can live with myself.

Parents' Walk About
Gayle Roberts

"I never thought I would see a woman teaching high school physics," the elderly man said as he was about to leave my classroom. I had just finished a ten-minute talk at Parents' Walk About, discussing the content of the senior physics course and the manner in which I evaluate my students. I assumed that his son or daughter was a student in my class, but, given his apparent age, I wondered if the student was his grandchild. "I don't believe there were any girls in my high school physics classes, and there certainly were no women physics teachers in those days. You're a good role model for the girls," he concluded as he walked out of my classroom and presumably headed for his child's next teacher and subject class.

The elderly man's comments left me with mixed feelings. Initially, I was pleased. After all, who wouldn't want to be a positive role model if given the chance? But for a moment, I had wondered whether his comments about my being a woman were motivated by his awareness that I was Vancouver School Board's first and, at that time, only transsexual teacher. I just didn't want to go there! My concern was not unfounded as the previous school year I was a male teacher, but after three weeks of teaching in September, I had to take leave to transition. Now I was a woman teacher—at least judging from the clothes I was wearing: a tailor-made skirt and jacket, a stylish blouse and makeup and jewellery. Did the elderly man know that I had been a man? Or had he seen past what some people may have taken as a superficial appearance as a woman and picked up the difficult, if not impossible, to hide male characteristics of a deep voice, large hands, and relatively larger stature. But pleasantly, after a moment's thought, I concluded that he had taken me as a natal woman, or, if he had known about my previous life as a man, he was too much of a gentleman to discuss anything so personal about me. With that realization, I replied to his comments as he left my classroom, "Thank you. I always try to be a positive role model."

As I waited five minutes for the next set of parents to arrive at my classroom for a repeat discussion of course content and student evaluation, I reflected on my current students, some of whom I had taught the previous school year for three weeks, but the majority of whom never had me as a teacher but knew of me by reputation. Naturally enough, that reputation included their awareness that I had been a male teacher the previous year. Such momentous changes in one's life, especially in a school, do not pass unnoticed. My fears of rejection, it turned out, were unwarranted. The only difference seemed to be that some of my previous students from the year before came up to me during class time, ostensibly for help with an assignment or clarification on how to do an experiment, and quietly said to me as I sat at my desk, "You're very brave." Another told me, "You're an inspiration."

The ultimate compliment at Parents' Walk About came from the mother of one of my male students of some three or four years earlier. After she had heard my, by now, almost automatic speech, she turned to walk out of my classroom, paused by the door and then walked back into the room, introduced herself, and then after telling me her son's name asked me if I remembered him. I told her that I did and asked how and what he now was doing. "He's graduating from UBC this coming spring," she replied. I asked her to pass my congratulations on to her son. "I'm so glad you have decided to continue teaching at Lord Byng after your absence last year," she continued. "My daughter is in your Physics 11 class." I thanked her for her kind comments as she turned and walked back to the classroom door where she paused for a moment, turned to face me and said, "You look very pretty," and then she was gone. I was overwhelmed. In just a few words she had demonstrated that she knew I had transitioned the previous school year, was a teacher whose skills she respected, and she completely accepted me as a trans woman.

Later that evening after all the parents and student assistants had left the building, I found myself completely alone in one of the hallways that led to the school's parking lot. Now I knew what it feels like to walk a few inches above the floor. And most importantly, after a lifetime of feeling shame for wanting to be a girl and a woman, I was at last proud of who I am.

All My Art Schools
Nancy Strider

As I sat down to grind out my own Artist Statement, I thought I'd get inspired by reading another one written by a future fellow Resident. His first few words filled me with dread: "Last year, when my work was shown in the Canadian Pavilion at the Venice Biennale . . ." Oh oh.

It was 2002, and I was preparing for a seven-week International Thematic Residency at the Banff Centre. I'd been gobsmacked when they'd accepted my application, mystified when I was given some scholarship money. But now I was experiencing cold feet—right up to my armpits. Would it really be worth it to get there and then be rejected and shamed as an outsider? Had they even read my CV before they accepted my project? Needing to get this straight right now, I picked up the phone and called the Banff Centre.

"I'm not at all sure I belong at this level," I said to the person on the phone. "Did I make it clear on my application that I'm not even an art school graduate? That I'm an accountant and mother who does art after I get home from work? I've only had one year of official art school, in Calgary, and that was thirty years ago, when I was twenty-one."

"Yes. But it says right here that you got the award as most promising first-year student."

"Well, yes, I did. But then I dropped out."

"Well, you obviously got an education somewhere. I'm looking at your project proposal right now. Our committee loved it. It is a good fit for our theme. Trust me, it will be fine. But I need your statement right away!"

So, I hung up the phone and called my old friend Twyla to help me write it. She knew me from the seventies in Toronto, where I'd moved from Calgary to start out as a freelance artist. I continued getting an art education—sort of—just not an official one. Twyla and I had met at a day job as 'plant ladies' in downtown offices while we prioritized our creative lives. Twyla had gone on to teach philosophy at a university. I asked her to help me to reframe and articulate my experience into ArtSpeak.

During the time we were watering office plants, I was taking drop-in courses at the Three Schools of Art, which called itself "The Other Art School" in contrast to the Ontario College of Art. Long on dust bunnies and short on pretention, Three Schools had emerged from the Free School Movement of the sixties. There were no credits being granted nor degrees being offered. Courses were cheap, but often taught by people without formal qualifications.

Founded on idealistic, interdisciplinary principals, the original three schools had been theatre, visual art, and something else. Nobody could remember what the third school was, it had simply withered when nobody signed up. Hierarchical lines were intentionally blurred. One year, there was big excitement when someone returned from a gig in a musical and offered to teach tap dancing. Students, teachers, administrators, models, even the guy who ran the bookstore on the corner, all signed up to tap. In the daily life-drawing drop-in class, if the model didn't show up, one of us regulars would just take a turn stripping and standing on the podium. At the end of the session we'd wander around, commenting on each other's work, most of which would be casually tossed in the garbage as we walked out.

The year the school was slipping into inevitable bankruptcy, we held a series of fundraisers. We sold Christmas trees in a nearby lot. I collected donations with a 'craft afternoon' in the foyer. We invited the neighbourhood to come make paper chains and other decorations, which we paraded outside to decorate the left-over 'Charlie Brown' trees. Despite additional hot chocolate revenue, Three Schools still went down, but with pride. They bragged that we students had sought 'learning for its own sake', and that not a single graduate had stooped to become a Celebrity Art Star.

Being part of that elastic and egalitarian institution had given me just enough structure to take myself seriously and to trust my gut about the art I produced. It was this very gut that was now churning as I faced trying to summarize myself for the Banff Centre, and for the art stars that might be my fellow residents.

Twyla suggested that we reframe my Three Schools years as "Strider participated in the radical and interdisciplinary exploration of alternative non-institutional community-engaged learning. An early practitioner of the relational and celebration art forms, she twinned her research, exploring both urban rituals and collaborative body representations."

"What a crock," I said.

But Twyla pointed out, "It's just a description of what you lived, made to sound more intentional. And no more brain-numbing than what I see around me in my department. That's academia for you. Swimming with the sharks." So, I took a breath, and dived in.

My Artist Statement got in under the wire, and I went on to flourish at the Banff Centre for those seven weeks. We residents ate in the same dining room as people from concurrent conferences, and our large round tables would be identified by signs that said 'Artists'. At last I had proof that I was one. It seemed that my memorabilia project was being accepted and appreciated. 'Biennale Guy', visiting me while I was conceptually flailing around in my studio, declared my process "interesting," and suggested that my Artist Talk "amplify the performative aspects of your uncertainty." I followed his advice. Onstage, whipping a sheet off a decorated and brightly-lit Christmas tree, I proceeded to analyze it as a "secular household shrine to nostalgia."

A highlight of the residency for me was the way that the artists would cross paths in the Centre's pub. One evening Biennale Guy showed up as I was opening a letter from Emily Carr Institute of Art and Design.

"I guess it's my acceptance letter," I said.

"A job offer?"

"No. I've applied to be a student."

"But they aren't even a university. They only do Bachelor's programs."

"That's what I'm going for," I said, "an official degree from a recognized art school. I'm loving being here in Banff, engaged in 'exploration mode' again. My son's in college now, and he's pointing out to me that he's virtually launched, and that I should get a life. I'm figuring I'll give myself the four years of an art degree as a reward for doing the breadwinner thing for so long." I ordered a beer, ripped open the envelope, and scanned it quickly. Then I read it again, slowly. Finally, I spoke. "They turned me down."

"What?" said Biennale Guy. "A rejection letter to first-year art school? Mailed to you here? While you are on an International Residency at the Banff Centre? You already got yourself here, before you even got yourself there. What are they thinking?"

"I suspect that they are thinking that I can't read. I didn't put much effort into my application," I admitted. "I was so full of myself for getting accepted here that I barely paid any attention to the portfolio elements they listed. I remember now they asked that I submit a sketch book, and I just skipped that part. Now I realize I was probably throwing away points."

"Who does sketch books anymore?" Biennale Guy asked.

"Apparently people who demonstrate that they can follow instructions. No doubt there were a few all-nighter sketchbooks, submitted complete with faux coffee stains. That'll teach me."

"Well that's my point," he said. "Going to school just teaches you how to please the bosses. All those grades. How can anyone assign points to a piece of art? Let alone to the student that made it? Comparing them to each other like they were a bunch of junior accountants climbing the corporate ladder."

"Well, actually, I am an accountant. Didn't you even read my CV?" I asked.

"Oh yeah. Right. Sorry. But you bring your other life as another lens, like you have double vision. I see you taking bean-counting on the road, detourning all those boring tropes, and making art with it. Surely you don't want to become just another BFA."

"Maybe I do. And don't you have a PhD? Right now, I'm just a midnight artist, here for seven weeks, living my dream, using all my vacation and overtime. I want to get out of that grind and get back to work as an artist. When I've got an assignment with a deadline, I do the work. Going to art school would rev me up and get me back into the habit. I'd feel like it would be permission to take myself and my art seriously again. For ten years, I've lived only a five-minute walk from Emily Carr. I've been so busy being a mom and an employee and a householder, that I've walked right by with blinkers on so I wouldn't see it. Now I want to have one of those student cards that you stick into the slot at the entrance, and a little green light flashes, and the doors swing open—day or night. To me, that would feel like the keys to the kingdom." I ordered another beer. "I'm going to apply again."

Over the next months, I used the application as my marching orders. It was reminiscent of my street-artist days to create a sketch book where all the coffee stains were earned. The next mail I got back from Emily Carr was an acceptance letter. I later found out that this second try at an application had placed me among their first picks.

I look back on those student years at Emily Carr as the most fun I've ever had. I stretched my degree out as long as I could. Living so close by, I practically wore out that student card. I was on a first-name basis with all the security guards, who would come by nightly to the studio to gently throw me out, so they could lock the school and go home.

In 2008, at the age of fifty-seven, I graduated with the Governor General's Silver Medal for the best GPA in the graduating class. Nobody believed that I was surprised. But I had been so focused on making the most of being there, and was so busy enjoying myself, that I hadn't been comparing my marks to anybody else. I had always agreed with Biennale Guy that marks aren't the best way of measuring an emerging artist. I had worked beside inspired students who were choosing not to do those extra steps needed to transmute their talent and inspiration into grades. Some were too busy trying to become celebrity art stars. But many were taking the same 'learning for its own sake' attitude that had served me well at Three Schools when I was their age and was chucking out my afternoon's work at the end of most life-drawing sessions.

Maybe there is some truth to the platitude 'Education is wasted on the young'. It had been my long years of showing up for ordinary life as an ordinary grown-up that had primed me to come back and tap-dance my way through a real art school.

Dancing Bear
Judy Fletcher

At an early age I learned that if you make them laugh they let you stay or at least they let you come back.

A DIALOGUE IN FOUR PARTS

Presented by members of Quirk-e's Memoir Small Group
at the Senior Arts & Health Showcase
Roundhouse Community Arts and
Recreation Centre, Vancouver, BC
June 1, 2019

Child's Play
Gayle Roberts

School doors open with a bang
The playground fills
groups of boys and groups of girls
never to mix

Boys at play
Pushing and shoving
bossy boys
"I'm next get lost."
cursing boys
"Its my turn God damn it."
fighting boys
"Oh yer whatcha gonna do about it."

I was one of them
a cursing sometimes fighting boy
independent
competitive

Girls at play
"Let's play on the swings"
"And then on the slide."
"You'll love the monkey bars."
"And what about the roundabout?"

Often in my mind
but forever unspoken
forever hidden
the wish for the spirited play of girls
sharing
cooperative

Girls at play
for them I am unseen
ignored
unknown

For me
unaccepted
alone
the wish to be one of them.

Who Knew?
Cyndia Cole

Who knew
a person like me,
born wrong
cursed as too independent
and strong willed,
would finally
come to love?

Not rollercoaster love
with thrills before the crash,
but love that lasts,
love that's home,
love that just is
everyday ordinary
and unbelievable

Who knew
all that Sturm und Drang before you
would teach me
what love is not,
and then lead me
through my true self
and the cosmos of my heart
to reach you across the universe
and at the water cooler
now twenty-five years and more?

Who knew?

Too Much
Lari Souza

I stared straight into her eyes,
looking for an answer to a question I hadn't yet asked,
with tears running down my face,
I hoped she would understand.

I didn't want to ask that question out loud,
I was scared,
I was terrified.
Why could she not tell?

I continued to stare hopelessly at her,
Hoping for if not an answer,
A smile, empathy or some sort of love.

None had been given.
Had I asked for too much?

Generations
Richard Brail

Lari told us that his poem *Too Much* was about his mother. It made me think of my parents, my father and stepmother, particularly my father. Lari, did you want to ask her about being queer? Was that the question that you wanted to ask your mother?

Sometimes that is the last thing that a parent will think of. Especially in my era when invisibility was perhaps our greatest curse. Or, at least right up there with criminality, psychiatric abuse, and a pervading culture of hatred. If it occurred to my parents that I was gay, I can only surmise that denial kicked in because they never said anything to me or anyone else as far as I know. One wonders how they did it. I walked in gay pride marches. Did they miss the coverage? I was the one holding the banner at the head of the march. I appeared on the TV news acting for AIDS Vancouver. Yes, they saw that, they told me. I guess they thought that AIDS Vancouver was just another client. One time, my father dropped something off at my house when I was not home and left a note "I was here" on, I guess, the first piece of paper he could find, a program for the gay film festival. Did he wonder why I had the program? I never asked, and I will never know what he thought, if anything.

And what about me? Why didn't I sit them down and ask the question? Like you, I think it was fear, maybe terror. We were invisible because we were afraid, and we had lots to be afraid of.

For a long time after my father died, I regretted that I had not asked him more about himself, about what he thought and felt, what his life was like. I think that many people when they get older, and are no longer preoccupied with career or other commitments or concerns, find themselves thinking about the past and the persons who populate their past, parents in particular, and regret that they did not take the time to find out more about them while they were alive. But I tried. At least once. I took my father out to lunch on his seventy-fifth birthday to ask him about himself and about my mother, who had died when I was three years old. It was like talking to Mount Rushmore. He simply was unwilling or unable to talk about himself.

Instead of regret over missed opportunities for direct communication, I have come to realize that I can reconstruct a lot of what they, my parents, thought and felt simply by thinking about what they said and did over the many years that I knew them. I can think about childhood incidents with new eyes. Also, I can piece together information from different sources. What did they say? Casual comments over the dinner table or in front of the television. One time, they were watching a TV program where the word heterosexual came up. They didn't know what that meant. They lived in a world where there was no alternative to their sexuality. Also, photos tell us a lot. Who is in the photo? Who is not in the photo? What is the occasion? What kind of man does my father appear to be in the photo? Athletic, outdoorsy, studious, thoughtful? One photo has him with a cigar and swaggering with my uncles. It was probably when my brother or I or one of my cousins was born. In another, he is grinning broadly, holding up a fish that he caught. Putting it together, I can figure out what kind of man my father was. Reading about the times and places in which he lived is immensely informative. Local histories, social histories—about where he and his parents came from. Even city directories are a wealth of information about neighbourhoods, demographics, employment history.

Back to being queer. All this tells me that my father lived in a world where queers did not exist. Or, from casual comments over the years, I learned that queers only existed to him as objects of hatred and ridicule. One time, when I was well into my thirties, I gave him some books about queers coming out to their parents. First person narratives. He couldn't return the books to me fast enough. We met for lunch, and he placed the books face down on the table, afraid someone might see the titles. I could tell that he had read about three pages. It was simply a subject so far out of his worldview that he could not think about it.

Did you ask too much, Lari? No. But maybe your mother was not able to give you what you needed at that time.

Richard Brail (left) Vancouver, 1983

MORE MEMOIR
Val Innes

Members of Quirk-e have been writing memoir since 2006 around various themes and projects, so it's no surprise that regardless of the small groups we chose to be in for the past couple of years, such as graphic stories, playwriting, or video, some of us went on writing our own stories. We all know that the history and herstory we carry from our lives as queers and activists has not been well recorded—in fact, until recently, has not been recorded publicly at all. We are, therefore, eager to tell our stories, to write them and record them. So, in ***Together We Stand*** *Queer Elders Speak Out*, the section Lessons Learned and this next section, More Memoir, contain stories written by those not in the Memoir small group. These stories vary enormously, from coming out as a young man to a psychiatrist, to dealing with dysfunctional families and relationships, working difficult jobs, and dealing with growing old. They are all personal experiences and interesting. Enjoy!

An Early Fall
Stephen Hardy

The sun was bright, but a chilly wind was blowing from the west as I walked down Edmonton's Jasper Avenue, turning north onto 104th Street. The fall was still young, with sun still warming the mid days. My mind was bright. My thoughts were happy as I thought about the upcoming meeting on this bright cheery afternoon.

I looked ahead at the concrete and light brown brick office building, a four-story walk up, typical of those early '60s professional buildings, housing lawyers, doctors, and so forth. I was looking forward to seeing Dr. Brain again. His office was hard to get to, first the streetcar trip across the High Level Bridge, then the bus down Jasper Avenue. But I wanted to see him today. I had many thoughts to tell him, many new feelings to describe. I turned toward the short outside staircase and walked up to the front door. I entered the building, smelling the polished wood floors and doorways, my eyes getting used to the dim lighting and to the dark stairway to the second floor.

I started walking up the stairs. Dr. Brain, I thought, a perfect name for someone who looked after people's minds, a perfect name for a psychiatrist. I had been seeing Dr. Brain for a few months, not saying much at first, but now feeling that maybe it was safe. I hoped it was, finally, because I needed that safety, today especially. I walked onto the second floor and turned towards the office, seeing the warm light through the frosted glass. Room 204, Dr. Julius Brain, R. Psych., etched on the door.

I opened the door.

He was standing at the doorway of his inner office, motioning. "Come in," he said.

I entered the office, looked to my right at the small mahogany desk in front of the curtains drawn over the only window. To my left, I saw Dr. Brain's brown leather chair, where he sat during our sessions. Beside the chair was the couch where I was told to lie during our sessions. I walked toward the couch. Lying on the couch, I could see the far wall, with a low table and a lamp. Books lay scattered about the table. The wall beside the couch was a dark beige, the ceiling above the couch a lighter beige. I closed my eyes.

"Last time, we were discussing your parents," he said in his usual low voice, devoid of emotion. "Do you have any more to tell me?"

"No, but I've been doing a lot of thinking."

"Yes?" he said.

"I think I'm homosexual."

"What!" he said loudly.

"I've been wondering why I have these feelings about other guys. And why I don't want to date girls. I like guys, and I get a charge when I see some guys in the showers. I feel like I want to touch them, to hug them."

"You're not homosexual!" he said, this time with anger in his voice. "First you tell me that your mother sexually assaulted you, now you tell me you're homosexual. You're making these things up! You have to get over these feelings," he said in the same loud angry voice. I'd never heard him express strong emotions, actually any emotions, before today.

"But what about my feelings for other guys?"

"Many young men have feelings like that. It's just a phase. You'll get over it. You're only nineteen," he said with a sound of firmness and finality in his voice.

My mind was swirling with feelings, doubt, shame. I just wanted to crawl into the corner of the room. The darkness of the room was enveloping me, as if I was just a shadow, as if I no longer existed in that room. I had wanted to discuss my feelings with him, to explore what I was going to do about them. But now, it seemed that I had no choice but to stop feeling, to act and live like other guys, to try to stop these feelings.

"He's a doctor, a psychiatrist, an expert on people's emotions, lives, sexual lives. He must know what he is talking about. I have to believe him," were some of the thoughts going through my mind. "What if I just do as he says, just put those feelings out of my mind, pretend they're not there, and try to live my life as if I were heterosexual? What would my life be like? It would be easier," I thought to myself. "I would know what to do. No one would ask any questions about how I'm living my life. My life would be easier. People wouldn't dislike me, wouldn't hate me, because of how I live, because of my sexuality. Other people, even my friends, would think I was just normal, just like them."

A strong fear started to envelop me. A feeling of being at a dead end started to build up in my mind. The darkness of the office began to overwhelm me. I started to feel physically numb, losing the feelings in my arms and legs. The fear that the office would close in on me, would surround and imprison me, became stronger and stronger. "What will become of me?" I thought.

Finally, I started to talk, but in a low, slow, monotone.

"Maybe you're right. You're the doctor. I'm only nineteen."

"Yes. Of course," he said in his usual emotionless monotone. The anger and forcefulness were gone from his voice. "Our time is almost up today," he said. "You haven't said very much since our discussion earlier in the hour. I'm glad you've come to the conclusion that's best for you."

"Mmm," I said.

"We won't have to discuss this subject again. As I told you, it's just a brief phase you're going through. I'll see you next week," he said.

I got up from the couch and left the office, into the dark hallway. The sunshine was gone, replaced by a dim light coming through the window into the second-floor hallway. I walked down to the front door, through the dark lobby. It seemed smaller and darker now, darker than usual. I walked down the outdoor stairs onto 104th

Street, and turned right towards Jasper Avenue. The sun was now enveloped by clouds. A brisk cold wind was now blowing from the north. Leaves were swirling on the edges of the sidewalk. I pulled up my jacket collar.

A young man was walking towards me as I approached Jasper Avenue. I remembered seeing him before. I remembered seeing his soft open eyes and his easy, inviting smile. I looked away this time, avoiding his eyes, and looked down at the fall-coloured leaves moving across the sidewalk.

As I turned onto Jasper Avenue, I was struck by the abrupt change in the weather just in the last hour. The cold north wind stung my face and eyes. The dark grey clouds seemed like snow clouds. The change seemed to portend an early fall.

My mood seemed to have changed like the weather. I still felt the darkness, hopelessness, shame, fear, that I felt in the doctor's office. The doctor was right; I was sure of that. But it meant that my life had taken a turn, a turn away from the brightness and hope that I had felt earlier today, a turn towards darkness, hopelessness, and fear. An early fall, for sure, an early fall in the seasons of my life.

Thanksgiving Chef
Don Martin

The first time I met my uncle Homer and grandmother Lillie Martin was also the first time I ever saw a live turkey. Homer raised a variety of poultry on his farm in South Dakota. He was a gentleman cattle rancher, never married. His Herefords were pastured up in the Black Hills. He lived with his mother all his adult life on a hundred acres of Dakota prairie near Sturgis, not far from Bear Butte. He raised not only turkeys, but peacocks and guinea hens and pheasants and ducks and geese and, of course, chickens. It was 1956. I was five. My dad and I visited for a week from Washington State on the homestead where he and Homer grew up.

Homer got up at four a.m. every morning, turned on the radio really loud, brewed some coffee, smoked two or three cigarettes, moved his bowels, and opened the door to the guest room.

"You gonna sleep all day," he proclaimed. It was not a question. My dad was already up. He was an early riser, too.

I stumbled into my clothes and shuffled, swollen-eyed, behind Homer as he made his morning rounds to all the poultry pens, scattering feed and refilling waterers. The sun was barely up, but I never complained. I was fascinated by his birds.

"I let the turkeys out to run around during the day and catch bugs," he told me. "But I can't let them out when it's raining. They're so dumb that they stare straight up at the sky with their mouths open to see where all the water's coming from, and they drown." I was just a city kid, and gullible, so I nodded and accepted this, but it seemed preposterous. Homer, I sensed, was like my father—his younger brother—a notorious bull-shitter.

"Your dad never liked turkeys," Homer said. "When he was about your age, one of our big old toms chased him down and pecked him somethin' awful. Whacked him real hard with his wings. Boogered him up pretty good. Looked like he'd been chased by a bear through a gooseberry bramble."

I had to process that image for a minute.

"Are turkeys really that mean?" I asked.

"Can be," Homer said. "But they can be as loyal as a hound dog, too. Their gobbles always let us know when somebody comes visiting." I was fully awake now, paying close attention to Homer's observations about the idiosyncrasies of each species we fed. The frenetic skittering of the guinea hens. The confrontational honks and huge, slippery turds of the geese. The flurry of startled ducks. The scream of the peacocks, which sounded like somebody was being murdered.

After the early morning feeding chores, Grandma patiently showed me how to collect chicken eggs from the nest boxes. She knew there were fresh eggs because of the chorus of proud squawks coming from the henhouse. Hens like to announce their daily lay. It was about the only thing Grandma could hear—she was close to eighty and nearly deaf. When Homer talked to her, he yelled everything, which I found unsettling.

Grandma had a trick she used to distract 'the girls' from pecking her when she collected the eggs from under them. She offered a bit of cracked corn in her left hand, and swiftly reached underneath with the right. It worked pretty well . . . for her. I would need some practice. Rather than duke it out with the hens, I waited until they left the nest.

Grandma fried up a dozen or more eggs every morning for breakfast and expected me to eat at least three. It was hard because I was a small kid, and I had a delicate appetite. She blackened the sunny-side-up, runny yolks with copious amounts of pepper, which was not my favourite thing. But she had raised five kids through the Great Depression, by god, and food was never wasted. You ate what was put in front of you, or you went without. When I meekly asked for less pepper, she misheard me to say I wanted more. I quickly learned not to be meek around her.

I learned quite a few lessons about life on the farm during that visit. When dad and I returned to the west coast, those lessons would soon come in handy. My family moved from the suburbs to the country not long after. My parents scraped together the down payment on an old farm house, which they spent the rest of my childhood remodelling. That first year on the farm was pretty lean. My dad barely made enough as a commissioned salesman to cover the mortgage payments and feed four kids. We had a big garden and canned plums and apricots from our trees. My brothers and sister and I all had new daily farm chores.

It fell on me to tend the poultry. I got up early every day before school to feed the chickens. We had ordered two dozen baby chicks that spring from Murray McMurray Hatchery in Webster City, Iowa. They arrived on the train in a box with air holes and tiny separate compartments. A couple of them were dead, but I raised the rest of them up to be healthy layers and meat birds. I wanted to order turkeys, but my dad wouldn't hear of it.

When Thanksgiving neared, we got a phone call from Homer. He was sending a special package by train, and we needed to pick it up pronto when it arrived. Turned out it was a big tom turkey and a goose packed in dry ice. He had slaughtered and dressed them two days earlier. It was cold by mid-November, so my dad salted the turkey and hung it up on a hook in the barn where it could slowly thaw. He put the goose in the freezer for later. My mom was grateful, I'm sure, for Homer's gift, though she wanted nothing to do with cooking this somewhat dodgy, long-distance turkey.

Mom was a good cook, but she hated the idea that wives were forced to do all the domestic chores, so she made sure my dad took a portion of regular cooking and cleaning duties, which was a radical role reversal in the 1950s. My dad was the more fastidious of my parents, a former army sergeant who revelled in barking orders to us kids. Because he was always ordering us to tidy up something, we called him 'Mr. Clean', though mostly because he was the spitting image of the bald-headed Proctor and Gamble brand identity. In addition to regular chores with the animals, he made us rotate doing dishes, dusting, sweeping, mopping, etc., and on weekends, had us 'police' the grounds of the family compound, an army term that meant to pull weeds, rake up debris, and restack anything that got out of place.

Unlike my mom, I didn't view cooking as a chore. I was showing an early penchant for the culinary arts, and the idea of prepping and roasting one of Homer's prize birds held great fascination for me. Grandma Martin, the mother-in-law, wrote out instructions for how to cook the turkey which she included in Homer's dry-ice package. This was the last straw for my mother. She knew full well how to cook a turkey and felt insulted, so, under the circumstances, she insisted my dad take charge of the bird. She would hover in the kitchen and provide a running commentary.

This was the first Thanksgiving meal I have a clear memory of. Its preparation would establish a contentious ritual that would last for decades. And I was usually in the middle, performing 'mise en place' and mediating.

Back then, we always stuffed the bird (it wasn't until years later that food safety experts recommended cooking the stuffing separately). Actually, my family called it dressing, not stuffing. Making the dressing was what always initiated the holiday bickering. My parents had very different ideas about the proper way to make dressing. Mom preferred the chunkier version featured in various glossy magazines she read, with sautéed vegetables, pecans, and no giblets. Dad liked the dressing to have a moister, finer texture. He insisted on putting all the ingredients through a hand-cranked food grinder before mixing them with the seasoned bread cubes.

Because Dad was put in charge of cooking that first bird from Uncle Homer, he decided from then on, he was responsible for every Thanksgiving turkey, and his way became the only way. But that didn't stop Mom from yowling, "Carroll . . . you're going to ruin it!" as each ingredient she frowned upon was added to the slushy mix in quantities she disapproved of.

"Stay out of it, Florence," he would retort. I tried to keep them from fisticuffs by standing in between and doing the adding and mixing. It gave me a modicum of control, though it didn't stem the war of words.

Before I go any further, I should mention that Thanksgiving was also my birthday. There is probably no worse holiday to share with one's birthday. On Thanksgiving, all the family disagreements come out—about politics, religion, bad marriages, and delinquent kids, as well as who should be doing more to take care of aging parents, you name it—and everyone forgets about you. The adults are cooped up inside for an extended weekend getting drunk and tormenting each other. And because two or more kinds of pie are usually prepared, nobody wants cake and ice cream, too. So happy birthday, kid.

Anyway, first thing in the morning on Thanksgiving, with the Macy's parade on TV, dad washed the turkey in the sink and put the giblets on to boil. He stripped the meat from the neck and ground it up with the cooked gizzard, heart, and liver, using the stock to moisten the bread. Of course, we always bought those prepackaged, stale croutons with the little spice packets, but we added more sage. Dad had me put two onions and four stalks of celery through the food grinder. The other ingredients varied depending on his mood and what else might be in the fridge.

"Oh Carroll, please, please don't put that in," Mom would plead, the second "please" louder and more desperate.

"Florence, shut your mouth before I come over there and shut it for you." And so, the bickering would begin and escalate all day. By the time the table was set and Dad got out the electric carving knife (used only for turkey), the luscious aromas would usually calm the tensions enough that my parents could sit at either end of the table and just glare at each other. The last bit of strife was among us kids about who got the leg, who got white meat, and if there were enough mashed potatoes and gravy.

That first Dakota turkey from Homer turned out pretty tough and dry as I recall, which became the source of another annual dispute: proper roasting and basting techniques. Every year, I studied Mom's magazines to learn the latest methods for the juiciest bird. As I became more confident and took over more of the prep,

I altered oven temperatures, put butter under the skin, used a foil tent or a cooking bag, roasted it breast down, or tried fresh herbs. I found I could allay some of the inevitable sparring by announcing I would be trying a new technique, so back off. Over the years I smoked, brined, bacon-wrapped, glazed, spatchcocked, deep-fried, and barbequed. I even made a turducken once from scratch with three different dressings. My interest and skills in cooking broadened beyond the holidays, and by the time I left home at age eighteen, with both parents working fulltime, I was cooking most of the family dinners. My repertoire of comforting dishes was a huge hit with college roommates and boyfriends.

In my middle-age years, my husband and I lived on a small farm and raised turkeys of our own. Homer was right about the loyalty of turkeys. Ours always let us know about visitors, and when we came home from work each day, they sprinted from the far corners of the field to greet us. We let them range freely and they roosted in the low branches of trees or on top of the chicken pens at night. We only ever lost one to a predator, a coyote or maybe a raccoon. But let me tell you, butchering, plucking, dressing, and freezing a dozen fifteen-pound turkeys is no small task. It gives you an appreciation for the bird, and the meal, that you can't get with a Butterball from the supermarket.

Mom and Dad are long gone now, as is Uncle Homer, and there is a bitter sweetness to my Thanksgiving memories. I can't say I miss my parents' arguments, which got worse over time and eventually ended with them living separately. I suppose being in the middle taught me negotiating skills. As much as I appreciated them, I couldn't wait to leave the nest, so to speak, and cook on my own terms. I have since learned techniques and secrets of cuisines from around the world. I take great pleasure in hunting down unusual ingredients, making elaborate meals, and describing them on social media. My friends tell me they are intimidated if they have to cook for me, but I reassure them that I am equally happy with a hot dog and mustard as I am with an herb-crusted rack of lamb. As I near seventy, I have come to the conclusion that simple cooking is best, and food should bring folks together, not force them apart.

Working Day Blues
River Glen

It was five a.m. as Jude made her way down the winter road. Another bundled figure passed her under the circle of stark street light. Neither wanted to be there. She arrived just as the cook was opening the back door. Barrels of grease and the dumpster laid a cloying smell on them.

With the harsh florescence burning the kitchen, Jude plunged her hands into a tub of iceberg lettuce floating in ice cold water. She broke up bits and put them in bowls ready to be served as 'side salad'. Back into the walk-in fridge, getting the condiments. Soon the tables were set, the coffee made, and at six she unlocked the doors.

The perennial customer brushed past Jude to claim her usual booth by the door. Jude grabbed the coffee pot and approached the old bird with a forced cheery, "The usual?" The bird pursed her narrow lips, and the hostile eye contact conveyed affirmative. Every day, I mean every god damn day, it was black coffee, one egg scrambled, and dry white toast. Never a tip of course. The cook gave Jude a sympathetic smile as she hung the order up by the kitchen slide through.

By seven, the other girl, Meg, started, and a few more customers trickled in. Meg, too, wore the scuffed white duty shoes, supporting nylons, mint green, snaps down the front, shapeless dress with limp pinafore, name tag and a nurse's cap stuck on top of her head. Jude smiled. Meg made it worth something anyway. And the cook, Joe, was nice. Then the manager, Bill, promoted to his level of incompetency, sporting his normal look of dissatisfaction, made a perfunctory survey of the state of things, poured coffee, and disappeared into the broom closet doubling as his office.

By eight, the railroaders off the Illinois Central filled the counter. Naturally, one of them laid a friendly pat on Jude's ass as she hurried by. None were tippers, but not even leaving a goddamn dime was criminal. No time to spare, tables needing cleaning, food waiting on the ledge needed to be served, three 'impatients' at a table wanting their bill, and a few more lining up at the register. Meg asked if Jude could make more coffee. The boss stuck his head out and commanded, "The bar needs a thorough clean before any one leaves today."

By ten, Jude's feet had hurt, and the endless circling she'd done must have been miles. She hurried to the bar area, the smell of the previous night's stale beer in her nose . . . the booze under lock was like a mirage beckoning her with an unattainable idea of relief. She sighed and set to work cleaning and then refilling straws, napkins, and garnishes. It was now or never. She took a quick break. Stealing a glance at the clock, she hurried. Lunch rush started mean and dirty here.

On she moved to burgers, churned milkshakes, and tossed an unripe tomato slice on the lettuce . . . a freakin' culinary masterpiece. Meg had an 'irate', shop talk for a difficult customer. Yes, it got Bill, Mr. Honcho, out on the floor, all obsequious, and siding against his server. Back at the coffee maker, Meg was upset and told Jude how much she hated this job. Jude nodded and said, "Go grab a smoke; I can cover you."

The place was a disaster, post lunch. More salads needed to be prepped, and the bathrooms were gross, but Jude and Meg magically set it all right. Even the cash came out even. One of her stockings had a big run, but what did one expect in a war zone? Sometime before two p.m., the shift was over. Meg and Joe promised to meet later at the dive down the street for a beer. First, Jude had to run to a couple of classes at the community college where she was, believe it or not, fully matriculated.

This kind of life made up the years during her twenties. As an old lady, it makes her tired just to think about it.

Grandpa John: Simple Treasures
Pat Hogan

He looks out from under bushy, grey eyebrows; he's wearing a bright red suit too big for his thin body, with huge shoulder pads that hang off his frame. His lopsided grin says, "Look at me; aren't I the cat's pajamas?" He shuffles into our basement apartment on Fairview Slopes, which has a view of the industrial mud strip that one day will be a thriving Granville Island. He's got his walking cane, and he's arrived to pick up my kids, Tai and Jaime, for their weekly outing. He's our Grandpa John, and we're making history. We're the first family matched up under the new Vancouver Foster Grandparent Program.

All I knew about John was that he had lived in some sort of care facility for years and had no family. He never talked about this part of his life. What little was known about John's early days was from Marge, the founder of Foster Grandparents. It was hard to tell what was fact and what was fiction with John. He was a storyteller. According to him, he was born in England, orphaned at a young age, came to Canada as a teenager, had worked in logging camps in northern British Columbia, drove a taxi, had a motorcycle . . . and once had a woman friend, whom he was fond of, but who had moved back to Australia, her homeland.

His life went up a notch or two when he was moved out of the care facility and into a bachelor apartment (all his own, he would say!) in the newly-built seniors' apartments on False Creek sponsored by the Kiwanis Club. Once on his own, he got a welfare cheque each month. Having access to money was a new experience for John, at least since the many years he had lived in a care facility. He called this monthly cheque his 'pension', and he was proud of it. He loved talking about what treasures he bought, what kind of deals he got. He was like a kid in a candy store with his newly-found independence and cheque! I remember those tales well, told with a pleased chuckle as he peered out from under those bushy brows, his head tilted to one side with a lopsided grin.

John had a bus pass that he made good use of, another thing he was proud of and loved to flaunt when he talked about his possessions. When Knight and Day Restaurant (John's favourite hangout and breakfast place) closed on West Broadway and moved to First Avenue and Boundary Road, John remained a loyal customer! He made his way to the bus stop, dressed up in a rainbow of colours—hat, scarf, jacket, umbrella, galoshes during the rainy season—and made the long bus trip there at least once a week for breakfast.

John bought a lot of junk food and plastic toys for my kids. I was trying to create a somewhat healthy lifestyle for my family, but didn't have the heart to say no to him. He was so pleased with himself! Later on, he became a foster grandparent to my friend's kids too. She wasn't pleased with these kinds of gifts for the kids either. She and I exchanged many Grandpa John stories over the years.

Somewhere hidden deep in the piles of my archived treasures, is the story John typed about himself, typed on an old typewriter he found, pounding one finger at a time on the keys. He talked about his life, his dreams, his woman friend in Australia. He wrote of things that he remembered and things that he made up, I'm sure. Somehow, I inherited his black furry toque which was his favourite hat during cold winter months. I can still see him trudging through the snow, big overcoat, big galoshes, mittens, bright coloured scarf, and the toque pulled over his grey, bushy eyebrows.

The last few years of his life, when he was getting frail and couldn't live on his own, he lived in a church-run facility on False Creek. And, even then, until his legs no longer held him up, he shuffled across the street to the bus stop, and off he'd go on a journey somewhere, anywhere, exploring Vancouver, even when his eyesight and hearing were failing him. He loved to wander.

What I didn't know until much later is that my son Tai, then in his twenties, on his many travels through Vancouver from somewhere in the world, stopped and visited John regularly, took him out for coffee, played chess with him in John's bleak studio apartment and later in the facility which was John's last home. Tai was a friend to John, and John had few friends. John looked forward to these visits. Tai's thoughtfulness for an old guy who had been a small but important part of our lives touched me deeply.

When John died, we met Ralph, the only other friend of John's I was aware of. Ralph was a younger man who took John out regularly. I figured he might have been asked by Social Services to spend time with John. These two bonded over the years. The three of us—Tai, me, and Ralph—sat there in the funeral home on East Hastings, telling Grandpa John stories, after the minister sent John's soul off to heaven. It was sad that this man, who had eked out a life the best he could, exited with only a small goodbye party, but we gave him a good send off with laughter, tears, and a bon voyage. History indeed was made—for Foster Grandparents and for Tai, Jaime, and me. He was our Grandpa John.

Not the Right Time
Harris Taylor

We chose each other when we chose to settle down. Our careers took us many places except home.

―――◆―――

Late August 2008, I visited Paula in hospital in Toronto. Her eyes lit as she saw me. Her body lay still. So ravaged by Multiple Sclerosis, she lay propped in the hospital bed, tubes fed, tubes expelled, tubes dripped drugs to her blood. Her dry lips opened to speak nothing comprehensible. Tears of frustration and fear. Her thin hand in mine could not answer a caress or a squeeze. A monitor recorded her every heartbeat but not mine.

Then, I was a stranger in her room. Spastic, her head shook NO in denial when her mother and aunt said, "It's Harris, come to visit you from Vancouver." This was the first time that I understood. This is what MS can do.

It was the last time that I saw her alive. Her aunt agreed that her death was imminent. I kissed her goodbye that day and mourned her alone in Vancouver. Never heard from her family. It seemed that they wanted privacy and nothing but the distance of half a country between us. My Christmas card fell into the abyss. It was not the right time.

Back when we dated, we talked for many long-distance hours on the phone. Paula was in Toronto; I was in the Arctic. Then, she was in Toronto; I was in Vancouver. As we were both working, we could afford to pay Ma Bell, but we joked that for long-distance lesbian lovers, there should be a sizable tax credit.

Vancouver became my home after living in the north. In 1995, Paula lost her government job in Toronto and was diagnosed with

MS. Did I still want her to come to Vancouver and move in with me? Yes. I wanted to be settled down and happy. Paula's physical deterioration was subtle at first. A failed step. Weakness and falls after basking in the sun. Angry outbursts from nowhere. She grabbed the steering wheel as I drove. How long could I follow this wounded bird in the sky before I tripped and fell? Her four-year descent into madness compelled my call to her family. "I can't take care of her anymore. I can't take care of myself. Will you take her home?"

"Yes," her father said. But unspoken, it was not the right time for two retired seniors to care for their child again. Their now-disabled child was delivered to hospital upon arrival.

Late August, 2018. I heard the voice mail of Paula's mother—distant and controlled: "I'm calling to tell you that Paula died on May 24. Her ashes will be scattered in Cape Breton by the end of this month. It was her favorite place. Goodbye." A chair catches me. I need to listen again.

To her parent's voicemail: "I am sorry for your loss." It is not the right time. Her aunt picked up my call. "Did she die believing that I abandoned her? Do you believe that I did?" I sent cards of condolence to her parents and her aunt.

As the one-year anniversary of her death approached, I wanted to send her family cards again. Christmas? Not the right time. Easter? No. Her tragic anniversary? It's not the right time.

No lines of communication remain open. No dial tone. The distance—too far. It's not the right time.

My Femininity
Lari Souza

I have never felt more aware of my surroundings.
The black iron rod in the closet extended wide,
Holding sparkly dresses and pink blouses.

The extravagant high heels were kept up top,
Right beside the humongous make-up bag,
And a variety of hairbands, hair-clips and tiaras.

The glitter-covered heels made me desirable,
The feminine tight and short dresses
accentuated my curves and big breasts.

I knew I looked stunning,
It was clear that he enjoyed me too.
But I had never felt more pain and insecurity.

Despite all the colours, textures and
sparkles that I wore on my body,
I had never felt good enough.

That femininity was never my own,
It belonged to him.
And it served only one purpose:
To make me submissive to him.

He used my femininity and the vulnerability
it created within me to make me his.
I was desirable, but only to him.
He assured me that was love.

Love was my problem.
I did not know what love meant.
I did not know I had to love myself first.
I did not know I could be anything but his.
The lack of self-love made me vulnerable.

But the invisibility and disorientation
I had always felt came to an end.
I have learned that femininity has many faces,
And I created my own.
Only mine and nobody else's.

I have learned that femininity made me
vulnerable because it assumed I was a girl.
And I now know, I was never a girl,

Awareness and Love—Shame, Blame and Resentment
Farren Gillaspie

Dreams have always provided powerful insights into my subconscious. After a tumultuous childhood, I spent a lot of time trying to figure out the whys. My mother and I were constantly bickering. We were a cold family, no hugging or touching for us. On my sixtieth birthday, I thought, "To hell with it! I am who I am, and if it is necessary for me to know the details, then my Higher Power can just make the answers more available to me." I was tired of puzzles. As one of my mentors said one time, "If you ask, be prepared to receive!"

Several nights later, I had an unusual dream. I had moved away from home, or maybe more precisely run away, many years earlier. In my dream, I was in my old bedroom in my family home, except it didn't quite look like my room. My sister was with me, and we were catching up on what had happened with each of us since I had been away. I knew she was my sister but she didn't look like my sister. My grandmother came to the foot of the stairs to say Mom was calling us for dinner. My Protestant grandmother and my Catholic mother were seldom under the same roof. She didn't quite look like my grandmother either. While I was heading down the stairs, I saw my mother at the foot and, yes, she didn't look like Mom either. She was singing a cheerful song that sounded familiar, something about her wayward son returning home, and he knew how much she loved him, and he loved her. I was so filled with joy that I started spontaneously laughing. When I reached my mother, I put my arm around her as we bounced off each other heading into the dining room.

I woke up in total bliss. As I am often prone to do, I queried my Higher Self before I could adulterate the image with thought. The answer was instant. "That was your real family seen through love without all the baggage." I was on a high for the rest of the day. But that was not the end.

A few nights later I had another dream. I was having tea with my mom in a love-infused room filled with flowers and light. All of the heaviness between us was gone, and in its place only what I could describe as love. It felt like we were there to resolve something. The conversation went something like this:

"Mom, I have spent so many years being ashamed. At first, I thought it was because I was so skinny, or my head was so big. Then I thought it was because I was gay. But in this moment with you right now, I am drawn back to a summer day when I was twelve, and I was wearing some old shorts that I often wore. In a very firm maybe even angry voice, you told me to go upstairs right away and change into long pants, that I was too old for shorts, and I was being indecent. I am realizing just now that I thought I must be indecent and my body was bad."

As I shared with my mom, I could see and feel her pain.

"My dear son, you were not indecent, and your body wasn't bad. You were my beautiful son. I wanted to keep you safe. I saw you as vulnerable." She paused, "I know, I was that age. I was vulnerable, and my mother didn't protect me."

Getting Old
Greta Hurst

I'm so pissed by the fact I'm now old. OLD!!

I only realized this fact recently at my eighty-third birthday. Did I want to celebrate? Absolutely not!! It has taken several months for me to become aware that I had crossed the line. I'm fit, and I try to exercise every morning. I go to the gym three days a week (twice on some weekdays and often on the weekends). I pole walk at least once or twice a week, provided it isn't raining. Twelve years ago, I 'lost' my extra one hundred pounds and have maintained that weight loss. I can still do many activities that people much younger than I can't do! However, naps in the afternoon are a necessity, and sometimes I sleep for two hours just to recoup my energy for the rest of the day.

I finally feel old—a very new feeling for me. Not so long ago, I felt young for my advanced age. Because I'm involved in the community, my friends and acquaintances are much younger than I am. Until now, I considered myself in their age range because I am engaged in the same activities they are. I've been fortunate to be in a writing group for queer seniors for many years, and I believe I'm the oldest member.

Recently, I became aware I had 'lost' my memory. Short-term memory comes and then immediately leaves. I have no recall when it happens. I remember the people I see regularly and from the past whom I've known for some time. But that's not true for the folks I've met recently. They remember me and are astonished that I don't remember them. It's mortifying, and I feel very embarrassed when that happens. I especially feel betrayed by my memory loss.

Yes, I feel betrayed about my age. Yet I'm happy for all that I have going for me. I wake up happy early in the morning (six a.m.!) and ready for the day's adventures. I'm not so happy about driving at night, though. In fact, I often prefer to stay home and watch television. I do admit I pray for guidance when I get into my car. I pray out loud when I feel I'm driving a little too quickly. It doesn't help that I'm afraid of arriving late for the functions I go to. One thing I could do is leave earlier and drive more slowly. What a concept! My younger friend, whom I go to meetings with, feels I drive too fast . . . really? So, she does most of the driving, and we have lovely chats.

I'm older than most of my friends, and my contemporaries often have health problems and seem to break limbs. Moving into an assisted-living facility feels scary—living with people who aren't functioning well and are boring in their conversations. It all seems depressing as well as frightening. Am I vain? I don't want to consider that possibility. I'll just get my bathroom renovated, so I can stay in my apartment longer.

Feeling old is new for me.

Aging Out
Val Innes

The first of us to die,
the least expected,
Paddy went five years ago,
typically quietly, without fuss . . .
some lingering regrets
but time to know, with growing joy
amidst the sadness,
that she was loved
absolutely,
an unexpected gift in dying.

She left a lasting hole in my life,
but the ranks closed, and Quirk-e
moved on through four more deaths:
two, Robin and Bridget, long, slow
disappearances with all the pain
that brings for them and those who love them;
two more, Frank, gone east to die,
and Bill, with us ever frailer until his death.

And still we move on, a smaller group,
aware now that this attrition is to be expected
as people get older, more infirm;
some leave, others join,
it's a changing creation.

We are elders, with the accumulated wisdom of queer aging;
we are dying, as is everyone, but we know it now,
still alive and kicking in the meantime,

time is precious;
there's work to be done,
and stories to tell.

There's strength in that.

Section 2:
GRAPHIC MEMOIR

Graphic Memoir Group Process
Judy Fletcher with Val Innes

When Quirk-e formed small groups in 2017, some of our members wanted to do memoir through images and drawings, so the Graphic Memoir Group began. That fall, cartoonist and author Sarah Leavitt, who teaches creative writing at the University of British Columbia, conducted a two-hour workshop for all Quirk-e members. She geared the workshop to people who describe themselves as non-artists. She talked about her process in writing and drawing her first graphic story and showed us many examples of graphic novels. She had us think about defining a whole page and had each of us draw the 'shape of my day', which we shared in pairs. Sarah's advice was to always carry a sketch pad and pen, and start a comic diary—do one drawing every day, no matter how rough. She encouraged us to start with a short, contained piece rather than trying to produce a longer story.

After the workshop, each member of the Graphic Memoir Group did research in the library, in book stores, and on the internet, looking at different graphic styles and techniques that appealed to us. We shared these examples and discussed or critiqued them. Then we each chose a format to try. We identified memorable incidents from our lives and began to sketch them. Inspiration came during our small group discussions. Our sketches and illustrations were done primarily at home, then critiqued the following week. We followed Quirk-e's Contract for Critique to carefully give and receive positive comments. Every week, we shared our efforts and asked for feedback and assistance from the other members. Some of us worked with a comic-style story, drawn in frames; others worked on images to illustrate narratives they had written. At the end of the first year, we brought early sketches, composition samples, and final drawings together to show our process. They were displayed at the annual Senior Arts and Health Showcase and were very well received by the public.

In the second year, we began much the same way, working individually. Sarah Leavitt came back for a more in-depth workshop on 'comic storytelling' under Quirk-e's community arts grant. She encouraged us to try different ways of producing a comic or graphic. Our efforts were posted on the walls, and we did a round of critique and congratulations. We discovered that drawing well isn't necessarily an advantage for producing an effective graphic story, although it might help; there are many techniques available to those who are interested in this genre but shy about drawing. Sarah made the process fun and accessible.

The composition of our small group changed a bit over the two years, losing and adding members, but the group had a stable core and seemed to adjust reasonably well to those changes. Part way through the second year, we chose a theme to work on in creating our images that was common to all of us: *Messages Received and Internalized*. We tried to illustrate the impact that these messages had on us at different ages in our lives. We displayed our drawings at the showcase in June, 2019, and many of them are included here.

In addition to the images in this section, other graphics created by Judy Fletcher are sprinkled throughout the anthology. Judy has focused on illustrating her life's memories, and is a strong advocate for the 'I' in our Queer 'Imaging' and Riting Kollective for Elders.

Guest Artist Workshop:
Comic Storytelling
Sarah Leavitt

Many writers are terrified by the thought of making comics. "Oh, I could never do that! I can't draw." But as the wonderful cartoonist and teacher Lynda Barry would say, we all drew as children. Then at some point, usually around the age of ten, we learned that only people who are 'good' at drawing (or dancing, or singing or any sort of art) should continue, and so we stop drawing and get scared to try again. Huge congratulations to the members of Quirk-e for diving enthusiastically into comics class!

Each time I teach comics to a group of writers who are mostly non-drawers, I begin by trying to help them find their way back to the joy and confidence they felt when they were kids with crayons. Another important part of the beginning of comics class is examining all the different skills that go into making effective comics. Drawing skill is only one part of the equation. A lot of the work of comics is organizing content, figuring out how to divide up a page, learning what will fit into a panel or speech balloon, and creating a clear path for the reader to follow through your words and images.

In my first meeting with Quirk-e, we talked about how comics work and looked at some examples of memoir comics, many of which use very simple drawing styles that are accessible even to first-time comics makers. We then did an exercise developed by Nick Sousanis: "Grids and Gestures" (if you're curious, you can find a full description of the exercise and many examples with a quick internet search). Each person takes a piece of paper and divides it up to represent their typical day. They then fill each division with marks that represent what was going on during that time—but the catch is that you can only use shapes and marks. No text, no representational images. This shifts the focus away from how skillfully you can draw things like people and cars to questions like, what size and shape of panels will I use to contrast the super slow bus ride to work with the frenetic pace of my job once I get there? What shapes and lines can I use to represent how I feel in that last hour before bed?

The following year, I came back for a longer workshop, and the group really dug into the nuts and bolts of comics making. We started with a quick exercise to get everyone drawing characters and speech balloons. Then, using examples taken from published comics, we reviewed some of the elements that cartoonists need to consider for each project, including words, images, panel size and shape, and page layout. We then moved into the process of creating a short comic. We used scripting and thumbnails (quick sketches) to plan the comics, then shared drafts in pairs to get feedback before moving into more finished pencil drawings.

It's been such an honour to work with the Quirk-e folks; I can't wait to read the comics in this book.

MESSAGES RECEIVED AND INTERNALIZED

Child

Judy Fletcher

messages internalized

Are you eating again?

Why can't you do anything right?

People cannot be trusted!

I am scared!

I'm so fat!

You are not smart enough.

Be Afraid! Be Afraid all the time!

I am so hopeless!

I am stupid, stupid, stupid!

You should be ashamed of your self.

If I stay very still, no one will see me.

you never forget them

Teen

Chris Morrissey

messages overheard

- YOU DIRTY DYKE
- She needs to see a psychiatrist
- Dare I confess?
- It's just a phase
- Why do they make fun of me?
- Am I really sick?
- I'm not crazy
- Homos are a security risk.
- Why do they make fun of me?
- I don't believe it
- BE CAREFUL.
- Homosexuals are sinners
- They should all be killed
- Dress more like a lady
- HIV+? They get what they deserve

"it's hard to overcome"

Younger Senior

Anonymous Quirkie

public relations

- How much did that cost?
- Wish I could afford one of those
- Get out of my way
- Get a job!
- Fake! You're not old
- Useless trash
- My head hurts
- Die! I mean you Die!
- My hair is not grey - its my Silver Lining!
- Who do you think you are???
- Your wheels are my Tax Dollars
- obviously, you have bad karma
- Lazy bitch

younger senior with a disability

Anonymous QUIRK-E

Senior

Chris Morrissey

MORE COMIC STORIES

Good Feet
Cyndia Cole

New School
Judy Fletcher

So There!

Judy Fletcher

I had to sit by the stove looking at picture books all day.

Dear Mrs Chatterson,
My daughter, Judy, is definetly in Grade 4. I am sure that the school records will come from Trenton very soon. In the meantime, put Judy in with your grade 4 students.
sincerely
Sally Fletcher

NEXT DAY...

Me! Me! Mrs Chatterson I know! I know!

Christmas Presents
Cyndia Cole

One Christmas we had plenty of snow. But I had no dough.

So I went to the Library,

And checked out books on my sweetheart's favourite subjects.

- Horror Flicks with Queer Monsters
- Vancouver's Gorgeous Theatres Before they got Demolished
- Gravestone Poetry
- Hidden Gay Lyrics by Sister DJ

I wrapped them up all festive.

She loved the presents. But was shocked that she had to take them back.

I knew she would return them cause she worked at the Library.

Tommy
Judy Fletcher

one night, in 1961,
our phone rang at 3:00am
a drunk driver
had murdered
my parents' only son.

in the weeks that followed
there was a terrible silence
in our house.

my parents' grief was so intense
I sometimes thought
that they didn't want to live.
what would happen to me?

every where that I went
people asked:
"how are your parents?"

what do you think?

 their only son is dead!
BUT
MY big brother is dead
AND my best friend is dead!
AND
I'm scared

that I am going to lose my mom and dad too!

Fears
Judy Fletcher

Panel 1: A few weeks after my 30th birthday, I consult a psychiatrist.
- What would you say are your greatest fears?
- Dying!
- I was kind of short back then.

Panel 2:
- Anything else?
- Dying alone

Panel 3:
- Any other fears?
- Dying alone & being eaten by my own cats.
- ...and public speaking.

Section 3:
PLAYWRITING

Playwriting Group Process
Don Martin and Val Innes

Quirk-e has always been a performance-oriented group, so it was natural that one of the small groups to form in 2017 was playwriting. Award-winning Vancouver playwright and composer Dorothy Dittrich led our initial two-hour workshop that year. She urged us, once we settled on a subject, to write with absolute freedom, focusing on feelings and a sense of waking up to something. Good dialogue needs to match the characters meticulously, she said, and 'workshopping' the script (reading it over and over with people other than the authors) is a way to identify what is missing.

The Playwriting Group started with seven members. Recognizing our limits as actors and people who had trouble memorizing lines, we pitched ideas to each other and brainstormed various staging, settings, and situations that were within our capabilities. Then in November 2017, Prime Minister Trudeau apologized to the LGBTQ2S community in front of the House of Commons, and we landed on a topic—the traumas we had all experienced for which the apology was offered. These experiences ran the gamut from being forced to hide oneself, rejection by family and friends, losing a job, and child custody fights, to physical violence and suicide of a student and a family member because of government sanctioned homophobia. We each wanted to write about our own personal trauma. We felt we deserved an apology. So we agreed that the characters in our play would essentially be us.

That December, Dennis Sumara, Dean of Education at University of Calgary, held a community discussion about Trudeau's apology with LGBTQ2S elders in Vancouver. Opinions varied within our group about the impact of the apology. Trudeau vowed that government oppression of LGBTQ2S people would never happen again. We were not convinced. Governments change. Speaking out is as important today as it was fifty years ago. Our gains were not simply given; we fought for change. Members of our group have been political and cultural activists since the 1960s, and we continue to advocate for justice and social change today. This struggle between human rights progress and potential backsliding seemed like the perfect core conflict of a play.

Writing as a group is a challenge. We work by consensus. Initially, we conducted a brainstorming session where we plotted out characters and potential scenes on a big sheet of paper. We spent months discussing how the experiences of our characters could intertwine and build dramatically, but we got precious little dialogue down on paper. We worked individually on short, four-sentence monologues about our characters, which we turned into a 10-minute skit. We rehearsed, refined, and performed the skit at the Arts and Health Showcase that June. It was about a writers' group meeting in a café to discuss Trudeau's apology and the oppression our characters lived through. We got a standing ovation.

Dorothy Dittrich returned in the fall to lead a more in-depth session on playwriting. She took us through a workshopping activity using the script from our skit, and we discussed the strengths and weaknesses of our core concept. During the winter, several members of the playwriting group were travelling, so progress on the script was slow. Earlier we had produced a matrix of scenes for our full-length play with an arc of the action, conflict, and transitions. This allowed us to work in chunks with only the characters in a specific scene. Each of us also wrote a lengthy back story about our characters and their relationships to each other in the play. Three new members were incorporated into the playwriting group in January, one of whom had extensive experience in stage performance. It took some time to get back to a consensus about where the play was going, but it also led us to try the technique of improvisation as a way to capture dialogue. Even with all the absences, the group was able to write several pages of dialogue, which everyone reviewed and added to either at the weekly meetings or by email.

For our short performance at the Arts and Health Showcase in 2019, we introduced our nine characters to the audience as a sort of 'chorus line', based on the scene in the musical *A Chorus Line,* where each dancer is asked to say something about themselves. The Quirk-e Players in order of appearance were Don Martin, Janie Cawley, Farren Gillaspie, Val Innes, River Glen, Sheila Gilhooly, Nancy Strider, Pat Hogan, and Nora Randall. Their characters' brief bios, presented here, touched on the issues and conflicts in the play. Over the past several months, we've gotten much better at writing dialogue and now have a rough draft of the script.

Guest Artist Workshop:
Playwriting
Dorothy Dittrich

When Quirk-e asked me to give a workshop on playwriting, I was thrilled to assist in their project aimed at bringing their stories to life and to lead the group in creating a process to bring those stories to the stage.

There are many elements that need to come together to create a play. In our first workshop we focused on identifying those elements. First, we discussed the many ways to tell a story. While writing for the stage offers many freedoms, there are limitations, but, in general, if we can imagine it, there's a way to make it a play. Could we describe the play we were writing in a sentence or two? We talked about writing as much as we needed to write, without editing or criticizing our work until the story was told. A major concern of the group was writing good dialogue. A good beginning is achieved by creating accurate and detailed characters. What do they want, what are the obstacles they face, how do they proceed and what do they learn? We played improvisational games and learned from those games that as a group we tended to over explain and say more than was needed to tell the story.

Our second workshop was held after the writers had created their characters and had written some scenes as well as an outline. Until the workshop, each writer had been reading their own writing, playing their own parts. It was time to give those parts to other people to read. This would allow the writers to hear their dialogue, to hear other voices bring other interpretations to what they had written and to hear where the script felt alive and clear, and where it didn't. Content that worked beautifully on the page was sometimes less effective when read aloud. Often it was simply a case of needing more action. We looked at ways to 'show' rather than 'tell'. The beauty of a play is that we can see what is happening—we don't need to be told as well. Again, we worked with improvisation to clarify character and dialogue. The group learned through games as well as discussion that voices were missing from their play, and those voices were needed to bring dramatic tension and action.

Finally, I met informally with a group of three writers who wanted to write a scene together. They were clear what the scene was, the motivations and obstacles the characters faced, and they knew their characters well. We began improvising the scene with two members of the group while the third member scribed. This exercise was fun and successful and the trio took the improvising and scribing process back to the larger group to use as a writing tool.

Working with Quirk-e, observing the play evolve as a whole has been a rich and rewarding experience for me. I am very pleased with the way the group responded and how they have grown in their playwriting capacity. The stage needs their stories.

Script of "A Chorus Line of Characters"

Presented by the Quirk-e Players at the
Senior Arts & Health Showcase
Roundhouse Community Arts and Recreation
Centre, Vancouver, BC, June 1, 2019

DIGITAL IMAGE OF A COFFEE SHOP ON SCREEN. PLAYERS ENTER AND WALK TO POSITION IN FRONT OF A SEMI-CIRCLE OF NINE CHAIRS.

SOUND CUE: BRENDA LEE'S *I'M SORRY*, FADES WHEN PLAYERS ARE STANDING IN FRONT OF THEIR CHAIRS. LAST CHARACTER ENTERING HAS HAND HELD MIC. QUIRK-E MEMBER READS INTRODUCTION FROM THE PODIUM.

INTRODUCER

Nine members of Quirk-e are in their second year of writing a play. They call themselves the Quirk-e Players. Their play is set in a queer-friendly café and centres around Prime Minister Trudeau's apology to LGBTQ communities in 2017. Last year at this event, they gave you a taste of the writing process by acting out some of the issues. Since then, they have outlined the script and drafted several scenes. One of the challenges in writing a play is developing the characters. Today we would like to briefly introduce you to them. Honoured guests, I give you the chorus line of characters from the play entitled "Sorry."

INTRODUCER EXITS. LIGHT ON PLAYERS CENTRE STAGE. PLAYERS SIT. STARTING WITH PHILIP, PLAYERS CROSS RIGHT ANKLE OVER LEFT IN A WAVE. PLAYERS REMAIN NEUTRAL WITH ANKLES CROSSED UNTIL THEY SPEAK.

PHILIP

UNCROSSES ANKLES, SPEAKS INTO MIC

Hello! My name is Philip and I'll be your waiter this afternoon. Before I tell you about our specials, let me tell you a little about myself. I'm 66. My friends call me Pip. I've been a waiter all my working life, and I am really good at making people feel welcomed. I love this little café and all the queer and quirky folks who come here. And I love Vancouver. I came here via Toronto in 1990 after . . . my boyfriend died of AIDS. Somehow, I will never know how, I didn't get the virus. I was the one who watched all my friends get sick and . . . well . . . that's enough about me. What can I get you folks?

HANDS MIC TO SAM

SAM

UNCROSSES ANKLES, SPEAKS INTO MIC

Hi, I'm Sam, a 72-year-old lesbian worried about getting Alzheimer's. It runs in the family. I came out as a lesbian in my mid-thirties, after taking my kids and leaving a battering husband. I had to fight for custody of my kids because the prevailing medical and legal opinion was that being a lesbian made you an unfit mother. Well, it all turned out ok in the end. I have a wonderful wife, supportive children and eleven grandchildren . . . which may be a bit excessive.

HANDS MIC TO BYRON

BYRON

UNCROSSES ANKLES, SPEAKS INTO MIC

Hi, I'm Byron. I am in my late sixties. I have been described as a complicated stoic. My gay cousin committed suicide when he was

26. I draw from my life experiences in the flowery '70s, and the AIDS crisis in the '80s along with depression and a broken heart. Now I am bonding with my fellow queer writers and trying to release my inner radical.

HANDS MIC TO JAY

JAY

UNCROSSES ANKLES, SPEAKS INTO MIC

Hi, I'm Jay. I came out at thirty in Canada, and I was lucky—I landed in a great lesbian community and quickly became an activist. Hey, no civil rights! So no brainer! Decades later, after protests, marches, legal challenges, and court battles, we've got rights and same-sex marriage. I was delighted when Trudeau apologized to us for government oppression, but now? You know, he said it would never happen again. Well, after the whole SNC-Trudeau cock-up, we're looking at an alt-right, homophobic, conservative PM this year! So here we go again, folks!

HANDS MIC TO JULES

JULES

UNCROSSES ANKLES, SPEAKS INTO MIC

I am Jules: a self-proclaimed senior, cis gendered, queer post-sexual. I draw on my experience of coming out as bi in high school and spending my youth exploring as many ways of being in the world as I could. I have been in a heterosexual marriage and raised kids whom I am very proud of in their adult lives. Despite a disability, I stay as engaged as I can. I am interested in the evolving definition of family, the protection of rights, and the celebration of queer accomplishment and culture.

HANDS MIC TO RILEY

RILEY

UNCROSSES ANKLES, SPEAKS INTO MIC

I'm Riley, an old butch dyke often taken for a man. When I came out fifty years ago, they locked lesbians up and tried to cure us with meds and shock treatments. The lesbian-feminist community saved me after I got out of the nuthouse. I have been harassed, threatened, and shoved trying to use the women's washroom. The kick-ass activism of the Trans community has changed that for me. I am still mistaken for a man, but these days people apologize instead of beating me up.

HANDS MIC TO MIKE

MIKE

UNCROSSES ANKLES, SPEAKS INTO MIC

I'm Mike, from Prince George. My boss told me it's time to retire, and I'll be glad to get away from those office smart-asses. My wife, Pam there, is all hot-to-trot to "downsize" our perfectly good home for some Vancouver shoebox around here. The big down-side is I'll have to start all over volunteering in another Conservative Party riding association. I've put ten years into the one in Cariboo-Prince George, and now we own that seat. All that time, an NDP faggot has been walking away with this riding. But anything for Pam!

HANDS MIC TO PAM

PAM

UNCROSSES ANKLES, SPEAKS INTO MIC

Hi, I'm Pam, Mike's wife. I am so excited about our move to Vancouver after a lifetime in Prince George! And finally, I'm getting to live near my longest and dearest friend, Bette. We grew up together, went to the same church, were in girl guides, schemed and dreamed about getting the boys to notice us. Mike wasn't one of them. We're retired, the kids are grown up, on their own. Life is good! Bette and I are going hang out together like we used to. We have so much to talk about!

HANDS MIC TO BETTE

BETTE
UNCROSSES ANKLES, SPEAKS INTO MIC

I'm Bette. Pam is my best friend from the thirty years we grew up together in Prince George. When I realized that I was a lesbian, I had to leave to save myself from the popular belief that gays are sick, sinful or just plain wrong. In Vancouver I could come out to myself and the people I know. I met Alice, my deep true love, and we're getting married next month. I want Pam to come to our wedding. But first I have to tell her I'm a lesbian. (OTHER CHARACTERS LOOK SHOCKED).

(BETTE STANDS) I'm not going to apologize for being queer. I'm proud of who we are.

ALL STAND BOW TOGETHER. DIGITAL IMAGE CHANGES TO A PHOTO OF THE QUIRK-E GROUP. PLAYERS LEAVE STAGE.

Section 4:
TRAVELS WITH QUIRK-E
Val Innes

Travelling when you're queer can be more complicated than it is for straights. Even in countries like Canada and the U.S. if you don't conform to gender norms, travel can pose difficulties. There are seventy-six countries in the world where it's not safe to be queer, and there are more where it's generally safe, but maybe not comfortable. Completely 'out' queers have to consider whether they will be out when in another country. Partners may worry about whether they can hold hands in public, much less kiss each other or sleep in the same bed. Some Quirkies travel to countries where it's definitely not safe because they have the courage to do the work to help change sexist, homophobic and transphobic places into being more accepting. And then there are the places where it's fine, and it's good to be able to go there and relax, be immersed in a different culture and know that you are welcome just as you are. Here are some travelling tales to entertain you, some with difficulties to overcome, some with lessons to teach, some just fond memories, and some with surprisingly lovely outcomes.

Patted Down
Sheila Gilhooly

When barbara and I went to Ottawa last month to visit my mom, we had to fly, it being the only way to get there. Airport security has always been a bit tense for me. Having picture ID has not saved me from questions like: "Whose identification is this and where did you get it?" Or comments like: "It is illegal to use another person's identification." When push comes to shove, though, my ID does match how I look. But we never get to that point without several rounds of "SIR" which I feel I have to correct because it's airport security, and I try not to look like I'm trying to trick anybody. Since having three joint replacements, it has become even more complicated because if you set that bleeper off, and emptying your pockets doesn't fix it, you have to be frisked by a guard with a 'wand', a thinnish, electronic, billy club.

There were two guards, a woman and a man, and the man stepped forward and told me to raise my arms out from my body, he would need to 'pat me down'. I repeated, for the third time, that I am a woman and wanted to be patted down by a woman. They stood frozen, looking at one another and kind of furtively glancing at me.

It was only when barbara strode into the tableau saying, "This is my partner, and she is a WOMAN" not loudly but very firmly, that the man guard turned away with a shrug, smirking with relief, and went on to his next traveler pat down.

The woman guard was not happy and obviously not convinced. She approached me with a very hostile 'fine then, have it your way' kind of resolve. She pressed her billy club over and over my bleeping joints . . . hip . . . knees . . . back to the hip . . . back to the knees and then suddenly, right up between my legs and hard into my crotch. We can all only guess what she was thinking to find there (snort).

I felt that scalding sting of humiliation, but I didn't protest, just stayed standing there with my arms still stretched out wide in a bizarre caricature of 'welcome with open arms'. Then she started on my upper body and again pressing hard and repeatedly over my chest and breasts with her club and hand . . . like she couldn't believe they really are breasts. Finally, she finished.

She never met my eye and didn't speak until she pointed to a nearby chair and said, "Take your shoes off." She left me there and went away with them. I waited obediently until barbara found my shoes over on the x-ray conveyor belt and brought them to me.

We bolted out of there as fast as we could. I was shaken way beyond my usual crabby relief to be done with that particular joy of travel. I felt humiliated, and I felt like a failure for feeling humiliated. I'm supposed to have a handle on that stuff now. It's not supposed to bother me beyond annoyance or impatience, all with a real feeling of it being 'their' problem, not mine. And, of course, with my wit still intact. I have a lot of support and very active acceptance in my life. At these moments, though, I feel shamed at having let that support down.

But this episode has kept coming back to me. And always with a ping of failure which I realize is the humiliation still hanging on. I realize, too, that there is a certain level of their disbelief that makes me feel that I AM a freak. It's like a line gets crossed, and I have to wonder: what is so unbelievable about me being a woman? What is it these people see?

Sometimes, I think that my own sensibilities on the subject might cause me to over-read the 'you couldn't be a woman' message, but on this one, barbara got the same hit from the whole thing. As barbara put it, it was like the guard never really believed it and felt she was being 'had' in having to pat me down. Really, the kind of humiliation that a scenario like that would evoke would account for her abusive level of anger. All brought on by her own trans phobia, thinking I was really a man who had suddenly decided that HE was a woman, 'like they do nowadays', trying to pass. Though I must say I don't see my style as one that most would choose to that end. But it is maybe proof of the increase in trans consciousness: the guard thought I was trans, and in the old days she would have just seen me as a more unspecified, free-floating weirdo.

I prefer the stories where I score the perfect *bon mot* and leave my challenger feeling sheepish or embarrassed and me looking witty and completely together about who I am and how I look. And just when I think I'm impervious and won't get stung, it jumps up and bites me in the ass.

A Soft Place To Land

Judy Fletcher

When I was a kid, without any warning, my Dad would have a Grand Mal seizure.

Judy!!!

What!!!

Your Dad wants to go upstairs.

When he was walking upstairs, I had to walk behind him.

When he was walking downstairs, I had to walk in front of him.

Many years later I figured out what my real role was...

In case he fell, I was to be his soft place to land.

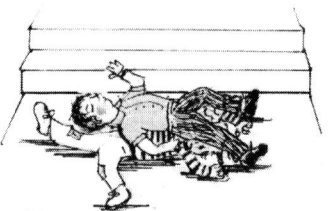

It's Customary
Chris Morrissey

"Don't hold the steering wheel so tightly," Bridget said to me as we approached the Peace Arch crossing, the border between the U.S. and Canada. "White knuckles are something the border officers notice." At least that was what we had heard. It was January 3, 1989. We were driving a 1988 blue Ford Escort rental. The trunk and back seat were loaded with bags and boxes. There was a full six-piece set of Corning Ware that we had purchased at an outlet in Portland, Oregon, a box set of cook ware, a set of cutlery for six, a TV set and a VCR from Costco in Seattle, Washington. Bags full of linens were stuffed in between everything wherever they would fit. We each had a bag of personal clothing. Having all this stuff added to my anxiety. I was sure we would be stopped. However, first there was the hurdle of Immigration, our primary source of anxiety.

I felt reasonably safe. After all, I was a Canadian citizen, complete with a valid passport that I had renewed at the Canadian Consulate in Santiago, Chile. Bridget, my companion, however, although she was a double passport holder, did not have a Canadian one. She had U.S. and Irish passports. She could legally enter Canada as a visitor, and that was all we could say. We knew that our intention was for her to stay forever. Would all the goods in the car cast doubt on her being a visitor?

The officer in the booth asked for our passports. She then asked Bridget, "Why are you coming to Canada, and how long do you intend to stay?" We had rehearsed this moment.

"I'm coming to help my friend get settled, and I'm staying about two or three weeks." This was not entirely true. In fact, it wasn't true at all!

Bridget and I were beginning a new life together as a same-sex couple. We were on a year's leave of absence from the religious congregation of which we had been members for 39 and 29 years respectively. We had made a decision to leave Chile where we had been working for the previous eight and a half years. We had been very closeted for years. While we had been in transition from Chile to Vancouver, we had stayed for short periods of time with friends who were lesbians and in relationships. The weight on my chest had begun to lift. We had shared stories, laughed, and relaxed.

On the way to the border, we had held hands in the car. "Won't it feel amazing to not have to be so careful?" I said to Bridget. Now as we approached the border, the pressure in my chest became almost unbearable. In 1989, same-sex relationships had no recognition in Canadian law. "Remember, we are only friends," I had said. Would we be able to conceal the glow we had begun to feel?

We passed the test, because we were waved through and directed to the area where the customs officers were. As we drove slowly toward the offices, we laughed hysterically. "What a relief," I said. "Good we practiced." I had learned over the years of playing cards that Bridget can keep a poker face when she wants to.

What worked in our favour was that the customs officers were not concerned about our immigrant status. The two branches were quite separate. As required, I had prepared three copies of the list of items we were bringing into Canada. One question I still had was, would we have to pay duty on all these things? I thought to myself, "We didn't do enough research."

The officer accepted my triplicate form and asked, "How long have you been away?"

I answered honestly, "Since 1960." I was seventeen at the time I left.

Without blinking an eye he said, "That makes you a returning Canadian." To my relief, he continued, "And everything you bring in now and anything you declare now to come later is duty free."

We got back in our car and sat for a few minutes holding hands. "Thank God that part is over." The next challenge was my parents.

They had met Bridget several times. They knew we were close friends, just not how close. We needed to stay with them until we found our own place. I knew we were going to face challenges, initially from my very Catholic father. That's for another day!

We drove the few kilometers to their house in White Rock, BC.

Spain: Famed Trans Singer, Falete
Paula Stromberg

Her naughty eyes and plump shoulders whispered, "Come here," across the marble rotunda. So, at the box office in the small Spanish village of Rota, I dutifully bought tickets to a performance by Falete, without knowing anything about her—enticed only by the come-thither poster. With Google's help before the concert, I was astonished to learn Falete is a celebrated trans singer in Spain, famed for her humour, for singing wildly popular songs, and for being gender fluid (at least according to her media releases and TV appearances posted on YouTube). I was excited to report back to Vancouver, to my queer arts and writing group, Quirk-e, about my Spanish discovery.

Falete is not a lip-synching drag queen. She sings in her own voice. An online reviewer wrote: "Falete lives for art—doesn't see boundaries between life and art, and embraces ambiguity as part of her lifestyle and sexuality—becoming an icon for liberal sexual and body attitudes in Spain." On concert night, my partner, Montana, and I joined a local crowd in sparkly jackets and neck scarves, who wafted ahead of us into Rota's municipal theatre. We were in the second row. The curtains opened right on time. Falete, wearing a filmy white gown and making dainty gestures with her fingers as she sang, was majestic. Thus, I was surprised that the audience began giggling—and then began staccato clapping the moment she finished her opening number. I could see I had a lot to learn. By the third number, audience members were leaning forward in their seats, hanging on Falete's every gesture, and sometimes humming along. Humming audience! We had bought tickets to hear Falete.

The heavily-perfumed women in the row behind gestured they were sorry for me that I didn't speak Spanish. Choking down giggles, they patted me on the shoulder as Falete introduced her fifth and sixth numbers. I can't think of a single North American performer who inspires audience members to lean forward in their seats with absolute glee dancing in their eyes, hungry for the performer's mere lift of an eyebrow.

As Falete sang for *amor delicioso*, several audience members shouted words to the next lines when she paused dramatically for a breath. A few times they joined in Falete's singing. The señora beside me in a leopard fake-fur jacket hummed loudly to several songs. I kept quiet . . . anyway, the señora had a nice voice. It was that kind of show: frequent shouts of *olé* from the audience.

Of course, I didn't understand a word of Falete's humour or her patter, but I did get her power of gesture. She has a magnetic presence. Flick of the eye, little pink tongue frequently circling her lips, a wiggle of one plump shoulder. I didn't interpret her patter as suggestive or lascivious—but rather as pure emotion. Concert goers' breath seemed to shudder with Falete's every song-sigh and whisper. Regal and slow moving, Falete seemed to be accepted for who she was: gender fluid, witty, and hilarious, yet capable of reminding people about bruises in their own lives. Her performance was deeply appreciated, but in my opinion, Falete certainly doesn't offer a Barbra Streisand level of singing.

In the second half of the show, Falete shared the stage with two tiny men, a piano player and an excellent elf of a flamenco dancer. Falete is tall, her giant pot belly hidden under regal beaded robes, with a round, round face. She sometimes sat on a black and gold-painted chair onstage, drinking from a crystal goblet while the bubble-buttocked flamenco elf made the stage floor vibrate. Proud, masculine, and miniature.

Falete caught her breath by the time the flamenco ended. She used the dancer's Spanish fan, a four-foot long, flowing red silk prop he left onstage, as her own muse—singing at it, kicking it, and shouting until her voice cracked over the blood-red fan. Most in the audience were nodding along, dabbing their eyes. I felt fortunate to chance upon this concert performance, made all the more enchanting because of people's gleeful love for someone as unusual as Falete. I felt people's hearts bursting all around me as she sang—I imagined I felt Spain.

The Resurrection
Marsha Ablowitz

We find Linda's condo in Jerusalem, and once we settle in, my partner Marie-Belle and I are very eager to explore the Old City. Linda, who has lived most her life in Jerusalem, warns us to be very careful sightseeing. "The old city of Jerusalem is a dangerous place to go on your own. A terrorist stabbed a tourist recently," Linda says.

"Yes. We will be careful," I reply.

Marie-Belle and I walk through the Old City stone gates. The Jerusalem limestone paving stones are hot in the noon sun and worn smooth by thousands of years of passing feet. All day long, tourists and pilgrims follow the 'Way of the Cross' towards the Church of the Holy Sepulcher. Some groups carry large crosses along Via Dolorosa. We follow along behind a group of pilgrims as they go through an arched gateway.

The white limestone steps leading down off the 'Way of the Cross' are worn in the middle. Descending carefully down the steps, we cross a blindingly bright courtyard and stand blinking in the cool gloom of the cavernous church. What a relief to be out of the heat. Do we have to pay to go into the Church of the Holy Sepulcher? There doesn't seem to be anyone selling tickets. The church seems to stretch away in all directions. There are curving staircases to upper levels and lower crypts, shrines, stone sculptures, fenced alcoves. Marie-Belle has again forgotten her glasses, so I am reading out loud to her from the guidebook.

"Here is the holy Greek Orthodox shrine. It contains the place of the true cross, the slab where Jesus was laid out. Downstairs on your right is the cave of Mary," I say to Marie-Belle. "Here, this hole in the floor is the location of the true cross." I mention to Marie-Belle that when I was in Jerusalem before, I saw competing locations of the true cross of the crucifixion and tombs of Mary all over Jerusalem.

Then I notice a group of young women in traditional dress, long flowing brown tunics, grey-brown head scarves framing bright, young faces, Christian Palestinian school girls. One of the girls approaches me, and she has such clear green eyes it's hard not to stare. She speaks softly in perfect English. "Excuse me please. My name is Fatima. What is your native country?"

"My name is Marsha; this is my friend Marie-Belle. We are from Canada, from Vancouver." She translates for her friends. They smile and nod. They have heard of Vancouver. One of them has an uncle who visited Canada. "Where are you from?" I ask.

"We are university students from Jenin. We are visiting Jerusalem today. Jenin is in the occupied territories on the West Bank."

"Oh yes, Jenin," I say.

"Oh, you have heard of Jenin?" she asks. "What have you heard?"

I choke. I can't very well say that all I've heard is that Jenin is a center of Palestinian extremism and terror, and that every time a falafel seller, soldier, or school kid is blown up or murdered in central Israel, the TV guy says the terrorists come from Jenin.

I say, "Um, uh, I've heard Jenin is a beautiful town with an excellent university." In truth, until this instant, it never occurred to me that Jenin had a university or charming young students. I'd only heard about the terrorists and killings. The young women are all smiles and nods as Fatima translates my description of their town.

Fatima says, "Yes, you are correct, Jenin is so beautiful. My friends say you should come to visit Jenin. We invite you to come and be our guests in our homes."

I reply, "Um, uh, thank you very much; it is it is very kind of you to invite us. We would really like to come. But we only have a few days here before we go to Egypt, so I don't think we will be able to visit your beautiful city." Fatima translates, and the girls smile and nod.

Fatima says, "We don't have a guide book. Do you think we could follow you and listen to you read?"

"Yes, certainly." We all step carefully down the smooth worn steps into Mary's cave. As I read from the guidebook about Jesus and Mary, Fatima translates effortlessly. We explore the tomb. The church has many nooks and crannies. We go up some stairs around a small shrine and approach a cool marble slab. "Here His body was washed; here His body was wrapped in linen, and here is a Greek shrine where mothers pray." Finally, we have all seen enough and head back toward the entrance. The girls are smiling and nodding at me.

"I have one more question," Fatima says.

"Yes?"

"At our college we have an American professor. He teaches English literature, and he is an excellent teacher. He told us a story about this man, Jesus, and we would like your opinion on it. He said Jesus died on a cross and was buried here in Jerusalem in a tomb, and then on the third day he rose up from the dead. Have you heard of that man, Jesus? Have you heard that story?" she asks.

I nod yes, but I couldn't believe her question. How could they not have heard of Jesus? They live just up the road from where the crucifixion happened. Was I totally wrong assuming that they are Christians?

She asks, "Do you think it is true?"

I choke. They are all looking at me expectantly. I suddenly realize they are definitely not Christian girls. Is it even legal for me to explain Christianity to a Muslim? I fumble. "Well, um, err, uh . . . that's the main story of Christianity, and lots of Christians think it's true. You know . . . like . . . the story of Muhammad and how he rode his horse up to heaven from the Dome of the Rock over there at the mosque in the Muslim Quarter." Fatima translates, and the girls smile and nod. I continue, "Well lots of people believe this story is literally true, and some people think it's a metaphor for spiritual transformation." Fatima nods, translates, and some of the girls wander off. Fatima smiles and rushes after them. I'm confused. I ask Marie-Belle, "Have I offended them?" As we leave the cool church Marie-Belle is chuckling. "You were a great help," I say.

"I was just amused seeing a nice Jewish girl trying to explain Christianity to a Muslim," she replies. We walk out into the blazing heat of the courtyard, out onto the slippery cobblestones of the street, stones that have been repeatedly washed in blood. I wonder if I will ever be brave enough to visit Jenin. I watch the graceful girls in their flowing scarves leaving the courtyard. They wave and walk away down the winding narrow street, turn a corner, and are gone.

God, whatever the hell your name is, if you exist somewhere swirling in our dark, cold, endless, random universe, please look down on your creation, Fatima of Jenin. Smile on her bright face, love her, and protect her from harm. Protect us and all our relations.

Melaque, Mexico
Cyndia Cole

Soundscape

Morning

It's 7:15, and a trumpet blares ta-ta-ta/ta-ta-ta/ta-ta-ta-TA! Sharp, rapid, military notes demanding I WAKE UP! Snare drums beat-beat-beat. Light is filling the high white walls and ceiling above me, but that blazing, red orb is not yet over the roof of the three-story, canary yellow house beyond the yard, through the rusted iron gate, across the dusty, cobbled street, above the open terrace with the white canvas curtain flapping and flapping in the breeze. More drums drumming. That horn pokes back in, insisting that I wake up, wake up, wake up! Now the cathedral bell is clanging and clanging. Can mass really be this early? The rooster proclaims himself. And all the birds are squawking, hooting, peeping and rat-a-tat-tatting, solo and in flocks. Non stop!

Noon

The street dogs running free, bark at will to hail each other and then sound off all together to proclaim, "We're here! We're barking glad to be alive!" Clip-pity-clop, clip-pity-clop, clip-pity-clop, horses' hooves on the stone and tiled streets thrill us tourists. And the vacas, the cows, with humps and horns, are quietly chewing and slowly wandering, not only in the ravine, which has a little water and mud and so is covered in greens for soft munching. But also, by surprise a vaca on la calle principal, Primavera Street! She is nonchalantly chewing on grass in the median as our taxi slows down over the speed bump. Suddenly, from the corner of my eye, on the opposite side, I see the other huge animal, only two feet from our vehicle. Despite the salsa music blaring and his cell phone call, our driver must have noticed because we are already past with no danger of colliding. He laughs when I ask playfully, "Las vacas o los toros?" I am delighted that I can make a tiny joke with my limited español and get a smile by comparing these enormous but oh-so-tame creatures to the running of the bulls.

Night

Only a day before was the last of the week-long celebrations for San Patricio (we have a single St. Patrick's Day) in El Jardín (not so much a garden as the central plaza). Bold young men performed the running of the bulls by dancing, sporting horned headdresses. The dangers here were the crowds and the firecrackers thrown at the indigenous dancers. Bang! Pop! Bang! Bang! It's a fiesta of music, always torrents of instruments, singing and talking. The sounds never rest, but when they ebb, it reveals the baseline ever present, the pounding of the waves. Melaque, Mexico, right here, the song of life, of earth and ocean, creatures and people, plays and swells and never stops.

Lesbian Meet Up

Maria is a friend and a Rainbow Refugee who found sanctuary in Canada. When she was outed in Mexico City ten years ago, her life was in danger, and her dreams were crushed by overt oppression. Maria knows Oxana, another Rainbow Refugee from Mexico, whose parents threatened to kill her girlfriend as leverage to keep her from coming out or acting butch. My partner and I are visiting Val, who lives in the coastal town, Melaque, three months a year. Val says she's cautious about being known as a lesbian but feels safe enough. Is there safety in being a Canadian tourist? It's our first visit, so we're feeling it out and avoiding public displays of affection, even though

I know Mexicans, especially women friends, are often much more physically affectionate than Canadians.

Imagine my surprise at being invited to the 'Lesbian Meet Up' at a local restaurant owned by lesbian partners, one an American, the other a Mexicana whose family has owned the place for generations. We sit out on the patio overlooking the beach and order in our mix of Spanish and English. I'm not sure how 'lesbian' we may seem to any onlookers. Perhaps we are just a group of eight older women friends sharing delicious food and delicious conversations. I have no idea how risky it is for the friendly owners to host us. I later read that despite some legal rights for queers, Mexico is the second most dangerous place in Latin America, with high rates of homophobic violence. Whether our Lesbian Meet Up is hidden or not, we are creating community, that precious antidote to the isolation, hiding, and silence we all remember from earlier years. Those women who return to Mexico every year, or who live here permanently, are most aware of how easily this suffocating closet can creep back, the walls closing in along with aging and dislocation. We are so hungry for the mirroring in each others' faces. As we exchange the rich stories of our activism to change it all, the winding journeys of our relationships, we are remembering who we are and creating the energy to keep on going. I am proud to reach out, to learn, to witness. Our little community claims space, even here, even in this land that has been so hostile to our refugee friends.

When I return home, I tell Maria all about it. She smiles and laughs and thinks of home. Hope is a spark that one day builds to a wildfire clearing away the underbrush of hatred. I am glad to have become one little flame.

Fishing
Chris Morrisey

"When will Dad be back?" she asked as she sat waiting on the steps.

"I have no idea. You know your Dad." Yes, she did. Every year it was the same thing. The family vacation was always delayed by about one day. This year, it was the same deal. He knew yesterday. Why can't he ever be ready! He made her so mad!

"I just have to go back to work to clear my desk, dear," her dad said at the end of breakfast. She knew that when he got back he would have to go and get the car ready. Check the oil, the tires, fill up with gas. They were always left waiting for him. Why? They only had one week, for heaven's sake.

By the time he got back, steam was coming out her ears. "Finally," she muttered under her breath. She slammed around as they loaded the car, shouting at her brothers when they started pushing and shoving each other. This was the one week of the year that they went on vacation. One week when her father's boss lent them his cabin on Bednesti Lake! Finally, they set off, traveling the gravel road for about three hours. Eventually, she spotted the three silver birch trees, the signal that they had arrived at the turn-off. They turned into it. Trees encroached on the pathway, definitely a "road less travelled." Finally, there it was—Bednesti Lake. She was the first out of the car. She ran to the edge of the lake, stretched out her arms as if to embrace it. Able to shut out the sounds of her family unpacking the car, she drank in the silence.

The next afternoon, she stood in the same spot waiting with anticipation, looking around at the tree lined shore line. Tall, stately, evergreen trees reached up to the sky as they had for generations. Only a few cabins dotted the edge of the lake to her left and right.

That day, they were empty. The lake was hers. She went back into the house.

"Oh come on, Dad."

"Do you have everything together?"

"Of course, Dad." Her tone of voice indicated that she thought he was stupid though she knew this was just another attempt at stalling. She had gathered the rods, reels, and the green tackle box and piled them up just outside the door of the wooden cabin. "Come on, Dad," she repeated. "It's time." Reluctantly, he looked up from his book.

"In a minute."

He continued reading. She looked at him, knowing that she would have to do more to get him away from his book and out of his chair. He was always busy doing something that left little time for his kids. She remembered their mother once saying, "He was never any good with you children when you were babies." Surely, since she was fourteen now, he would be more interested.

She stamped around the cabin muttering under her breath. She would have gone by herself if she could, but the boat and the outboard motor were too heavy for her to drag into the water. She went quietly close to him and snatched the book out of his hand. It was easy to snatch. This startled him awake. As she thought, he had fallen asleep behind the book. "Come on, come on, we gotta go before it's too late." It would soon be the perfect time.

Her father arrived, slowly pulling the sixteen-foot aluminum boat behind him and into the water. They launched the boat and, with the oar, pushed away from the shore. After a few attempts by her father, the engine sputtered and began its putt-putting as they slowly left the shoreline behind. Dusk was waiting in the wings. The reflection of the boat ran along beside them trying to keep up, never getting ahead. The water shimmered as the last rays of the sun tried to penetrate the depths. The surface of the water was becoming busy. Hundreds of tiny flies covered the water like a knotted comforter. A dragonfly hovered above the surface, the see-through wings buzzing. Suddenly it dived. Was it an early or a late supper?

They headed to the far side of the lake at full speed, which was about as fast as a souped-up turtle. There was the sound of another outboard singing back in harmony. She looked around; there was no other boat in site. She realized that the trees and hills were reminding them that they were surrounded by other living things reflecting back their sound. About twenty minutes later, they arrived at the desired spot. Everything slowed, and father and daughter prepared the lines. She had a brown fibreglass rod equipped with a ten-pound test line. She opened the tackle box, searching for a spinner. She selected one that resembled a trout, silver with an array of pastel rainbow colours. After attaching it and a lead weight to the end of the line, slowly she let it out, listening to the purring of the reel as the line sank.

For the next half-hour they slowly moved back and forth. Fish jumped out of the water. The haunting cry of the loon echoing around the lake occasionally broke the silence. It was an eerie feeling sharing this moment and this boat with her father. How was he able to sit so quietly? This was not the man that she knew back in the city on dry land.

She knew that her father had no control over the fish. They jumped at will, moved swiftly with the undercurrent, evaded any attempt to be hooked. "Bring in your line. We are moving over there," he said suddenly, pointing out a part of the lake they had fished before. He put the outboard in gear and sped up.

Once again, she put out the line. Within minutes, she felt the familiar tug. The game began. She let out the line, playing with him. Back and forth in a tug of war. She gave him more line. Let him run. "Reel him in," her dad called, holding the net over the side of the boat. They started playing games. In, out. The rod bent whenever she tried reeling him in. "Looks like a big one," her dad said as he got the net ready for the catch. In, out, a great fighter. Eventually, he seemed to be tiring. As she brought him closer to the boat, she saw how beautiful he was.

She took the net from her dad's hand, and as she lifted him out of the water, the fish gave one last struggle. Suddenly, there was a big splash.

"I guess your old dad can still teach you a thing or two. Next time, let me bring him in." The sound from the outboard increased as the sky and the lake turned pink. "Maybe we'll have better luck tomorrow," her dad shouted out over the noise of the engine. She turned her head and smiled to herself. There would be no trout for supper that night.

Peace
Val Innes

The blood red kayak stands out against the grey rocks, but glides gracefully into the water as if it was born there. It beckons, and I respond, grateful for the suggestion after a day of creating shelving and ten minutes of the latest news on another Trump disaster. Sliding it carefully into the water (it's my brother's and new), I am amazed at how easy it is to get into in a shallow dip past the rock edge. I settle, gazing out at this bay I love, the loons already calling from not far away, the sun shimmering in early evening light on the water, and the kayak, light in the water, skimming along with every stroke of the paddle. Why have I never done this here before? Canoes, that's why; I grew up with canoes, and you can share those, but this . . . this, by myself, is a miracle of easy movement, lovely through reeds, over the submerged rocks, over the underwater garden, by the beach and out into the centre of the bay, over to the rockface at the end of the bay where the trees grow out of cracks in the rock, miracles of insistent life. Peace, such quiet peace, and I am visited by two curious loons while I make my way home to my cottage, and the sun dips behind the distant trees across the bay.

Arctic Adventure
Harris Taylor

During the unlikely event of a snowbound winter day in Vancouver, my hands are cold and chapped as I place my Inuit carvings in the snow. It's my playful narrative statement about the north/south dichotomy that Canadians don't stop consuming to consider—unless they have lived there. From the dry crack in my skin, I bleed in the snow. Oh, bloody hell. It's an artistic dilemma— begin this project again in a pristine snow environment or go with the flow?

Go! Agency provokes me, as tomorrow the snow will be gone.

Life lessons from the Arctic remain in my veins. Ice, life, Inuit art are all part of a fragile ecosystem and a cultural testament of survival.

So glad that I saw the North Pole before it became the North Pool.

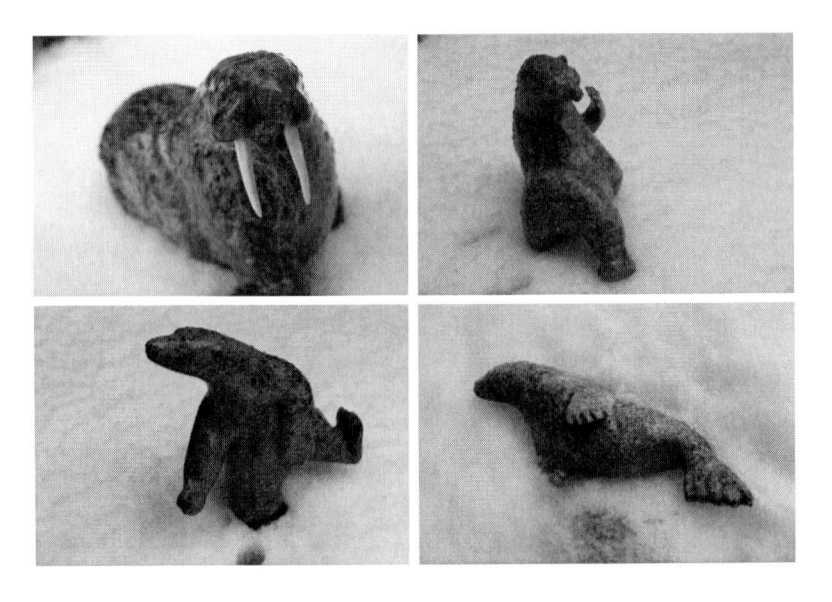

Morning in Glen Park
Nora D Randall

Seymour, my dog, and I are out for our morning walk to Glen Park. It's our long walk of the day. My joints loosen up, and Seymour usually gets in two or three poos. This morning because it is not raining, I sit on the bench under yet another chestnut tree and do the sudoku in the *Star Weekly*. The neighbourhood is full of chestnut and oak trees, and in the fall, after a rain or in a wind, our walk is punctuated by the ping and pop of acorns and chestnuts falling on cars and sidewalks. The other day, I almost got clobbered by a falling chestnut. It landed at my feet, and the conker popped out. I always thought kids broke into the casings to get the conkers, but apparently the chestnut tree has its own dissemination system.

This morning we arrive just as a teacher comes out and rings the hand bell to call in the children. The just arriving kids start to run and their parents increase their walking speed. On the play ground, there are four children and their minders who do not heed the bell. One of them looks like he should. He is tall enough to be in the first grade, but he is unconcerned as he swings, lying flat horizontally, supported by the canvas swing seat under his belly. He is wearing the full superman outfit: red boot covers, blue tights and long-sleeved shirt, red briefs and cape with the yellow trade mark 'S'. I think any minute, one of the two women with the children will tell him to leg it to class, but they don't. Maybe he is big for his age.

There is no doubt about the other three. The two that look like twins can't be more than three. They are racing around on their scooters. They are the same height, shape, and weight with the same blonde hair sticking out from their pink bike helmets, but they are not dressed the same. They do get points for matching, however, because the one with purple boots has a purple scooter and the one with pink boots has a pink scooter. I'm thinking they are surprisingly coordinated for their size, one boot firmly planted on the scooter, the other pumping away alongside. Then one of them falls and starts to cry, and the woman they have been circling runs over to pick her/him up. All is immediately well.

The last one cannot be more than sixteen months old. She is tricked out in a winter onesie that causes her arms to stick out like airplane wings. The woman with her has lifted her out of the buggy and stood her on the ground. The next time the woman looks up, onesie is standing in a puddle twenty feet away. I didn't even see her get there, and I'm watching the whole scene. The woman ducks back into the buggy and comes up with a pair of boots that she takes over to the puddle and substitutes for the now sodden runners. Onesie continues to stand in the puddle contemplating her next move.

I realize that it may not be raining now, but my bum is wet from the bench, and my dog is shivering. Time to start home.

Section 5:
TOGETHER WE STAND
Val Innes

Quirk-e is, and always has been, an imaging and writing group, but we are also, most of us, a band of activists whose experiences span many decades and many different places. We've marched; we've chanted; we've volunteered, worked with AIDS patients (outcasts to the rest of the world), worked on Pride, organized conferences or spent time being Rape Crisis counsellors. We're feminists, out loud lesbians, and gay and trans organizers. Living in the '60s, '70s, '80s, and even '90s as a queer meant fighting for the same rights straights have enjoyed all along. Fighting in the streets, in the courts, in schools and universities, at work, and on the ballot for the right to be who we are and to be safe being who we are. Here are stories of some of the Quirkies' experiences in those fights. Make no mistake, though, there's still work to be done, and despite Prime Minister Trudeau's promise that government oppression will never happen again, as governments change, that too may change. We're still fighters as you'll see, and standing together. We won't give that up. Our first piece in this section, Ellen Woodsworth's *You Have Struck a Rock* spells that out.

You Have Struck a Rock
Ellen Woodsworth

You have struck a rock.

We will fight back:
We are seniors, and we have seen the likes of you before. We will fight back. We are the rock that is there beneath the surface. We are the mountain that is full of memories of resistance, hell, terror, fear, rage. We are a mountain full of joy, experience, camaraderie, and passion.

You have struck a rock. The mountain has begun to move. We are shaking off our contentment, our patience, and our joy in the lives we have built. You will see us rise up.

There are millions of us. We have no fear. We have nothing left but to fight.

You see we are LGBTQI2S seniors. Spell it out.

We are lesbians who have emerged out of the women's liberation movement; we are gay men who have emerged out of the AIDS movement; we are the trans creating new movements; we are queers who have come out of the Black, Latino and Asian movements; we are the Two Spirit who have been honoured by indigenous cultures around the world for thousands of years; we are queers who were silenced for lifetimes, beaten up, tortured, incarcerated, and murdered. We are everywhere. We are the ones who created the laws that you are tearing up. We are the ones whose lives are at stake.

We know that life never goes in a straight line.
We are angry. We remember the past. Our time is short. We are coming out of our homes to join the millions of others whose lives you think you can destroy.

Together we are rising up.

I Support That
River Glen

The personal is political. The political is personal.
Feminist slogan from the '60s

It was 1969. I was in eleventh grade in Los Angeles. Did I understand what had happened at Stonewall? I can't remember. I did come out as bi to my gay best friends. We all fumbled about, trying to figure out where we fit in the world. I did feel I had a right to be me, and that may well have been bolstered by the gay liberation and feminist movements happening around me.

I enrolled in a sociology class at community college in '71, and the teacher was doing a thesis on homosexuality, so we heard lots about her research. Wow! That exposure was where I first understood what homophobia was. I mean, I knew my dearest friend was beaten up once and was doing his best to camouflage himself in the outside world as a result, but now I saw the systemic roots of the personal pain. I wish I could remember more of what I learned in that class. I do remember being in the Pride Parade in West Hollywood in '73. My social consciousness had been raised, but my poverty, poor mental health, substance abuse, and lack of direction didn't leave energy for supporting worthy causes. That said, I supported myself, got an Associate of Arts degree, travelled, and didn't wind up in jail or dead. Thirty years later, in my fifties, I would finally realize just how much internalized homophobia I carried around within me. But I didn't then. It was enough to quash my queerness for the security of being 'normal'.

Fast forward to getting off drugs cold turkey, and life in LA's fast lane, then moving to life in a hetero marriage with four kids, and farming in the Okanagan. I had no other family and only my husband's friends socially. So, when I became pregnant within a year of arriving in the north, I found the La Leche League which gave me the support group I desperately needed. There, I was surrounded by beautiful young women who were as high on creating and nurturing life as I was. I can't begin to tell you how much I finally appreciated my body and my femaleness after living all my previous life with low self-esteem and feeling I was second class in society. The group was a training ground in more than mothering, allowing me to develop group work skills. Over eight years, I became the leader, giving telephone help, organizing meetings, and doing public speaking.

The Okanagan was about as conservative as you can get, and most of the women in the League were no exception, so in the '90s, when I found the Unitarians, an epi-centre of open-mindedness in the community, I finally felt I could express my true left-leaning self. I eventually led services, taught the kids' class, wrote for the newsletter, and served as president. Most important, I experienced the process we went through becoming a 'welcoming' congregation for people who were LGBTQ, which finally gave me the courage to leave my marriage, come out, and to pursue a degree in social work.

During my university period, I volunteered with the Elizabeth Fry Society and an AIDS resource centre. I did a practicum in the alcohol and drug program while I figured out a lot about my own past, and I did another practicum at a women's resource centre, where in 1997, I started a lesbian and bi support/social group. I also went on the board of directors for the Okanagan Rainbow Coalition. We organized dances, put out a newsletter, and tried to get the mayor to proclaim our Pride celebrations.

I graduated with my BSW, worked in long term care as a medical social worker, and then I worked with the HIV/AIDS and Hep C communities. All the while, I was finishing up raising four teenagers. The relentless pressures I felt for many years eventually caught up with me. The fibromyalgia I had endured throughout my life took me to a new debilitating low, and then I got cancer. My biggest regret it is that I couldn't continue in my chosen profession because of my health.

The personal _is_ political, especially now that my range of influence is so very basic. I do lots of self care. I am on the social issues committee at a senior centre. I try to be there for my family and friends. And I use my connection to Quirk-e to support queer culture. I hope, in telling my story, to give voice and hope to other queers who took a crooked path to their identity, who used alcohol and drugs to try and cope, and who had periods where mentally and emotionally they couldn't cope. When the macro political reality bumped into me, I pushed back as best I could. Like the proverbial butterfly flapping its wings in this space and time and creating a hurricane somewhere across the globe, I believe I had an effect on society.

Socializing the Problem
Chris Morrissey

"What do you think we should do? Where do you think we should go now? What do you think we can do?" This was our dilemma. We were faced with some major decisions. Do we want to stay in Chile? For the rest of our lives? This was the question Rosita, our counselor, had asked us. Bridget's immediate response had been "NO."

Bridget and I had been living and working in a poor, working-class area of Santiago, Chile during the military dictatorship of General Pinochet. After fifteen years of dictatorship, the federal government was about to change. We were both members of a women's congregation. With Chile facing an uncertain future, we began to consider our own futures.

Bridget's very decisive NO meant returning to North America. I asked, "Do you think it would be easier for me to get a green card for the U.S.? What about Canada? Do you think we could get you residency in Canada?"

"I think we would have a better chance in Canada. We know about Canada's reputation. We also know how the U.S. was involved in the School of the Americas and their role in the overthrow of Allende that led to the military coup."

"I would like to spend some time with my parents," I said.

After months of this sort of discussion, we finally decided to try Canada. It wasn't as easy as we thought. First, there was the Canadian Consulate in Santiago. An officer there informed us about Canada's immigration laws. The only category that was available to Bridget was the skilled worker stream. She didn't have enough points to qualify. "Well that doesn't sound good."

One day we were telling someone about the problem, and she suggested, "Decide where you want to go, and go there. It will be easier to figure it out from there." So we decided to follow her advice. We headed to British Columbia and my parents' home. After arriving in B.C., we began the networking. We had met a friend of my parents, who one day told Bridget that she had arranged a job interview for her.

"But I can't work. I'm not a resident, and I don't have a work permit."

"Go anyway. It can't hurt."

"Well, I was offered a job. I can start as soon as I have a work permit. They told me to let them know."

And so the next challenge began. Needless to say, a whole drama followed. We decided to head to Border Services and see what we could find out. The officer asked Bridget questions. "What is your citizenship? What work do you do? What experience do you have? Do you have a full-time job offer? Wait here." After a brief time, she came back carrying a big book. Putting it down on the counter, she opened it and after a few minutes looked up. "You could be a Social Worker, couldn't you? Do you have $100 for the permit?"

"I don't think we do, but we can go to my parents' house in White Rock and get it." First though, we went out to the car, and we each went through wallets, pockets, even the car floor. Amazingly, we came up with just over the amount we needed. We went back into the office, and miraculously Bridget came out with a work permit in hand.

Bridget started work. For weeks, she came home from work to find me sitting on the couch, crying. I was the Canadian and couldn't find a job! Every year, Bridget went through the process of renewing her permit. One day, she came home and said, "The worker told me that this was the last time I could renew the permit." Oh, my god, now what. We had to figure out what to do next. Clearly, we needed a lawyer. On hearing our story, Mobina Jaffer, our lawyer, said, "We are going to march down to the Immigration Office and change this." She filed an application for me to sponsor

Bridget as my partner. The application was turned down. No such category as same-sex partner in the family class. I cried all the way home on the bus.

"I think we'll just have to go to court," I said. And that is what we did. "We can't be the only ones in the whole country who have this problem. Socialize the problem! It's not our problem! IT IS THE SYSTEM." That's one of the things we had learned from working with people in Chile. We found about a dozen of us living here in Vancouver who shared the same problem. And so the Lesbian and Gay Immigration Taskforce (LEGIT) began. We went to work: we filed a court challenge; several members made human rights complaints; we attended every public meeting when an immigration minister was in town; we met with Members of Parliament both locally and in Ottawa; we had conversations with bureaucrats, and we wrote and submitted brief after brief.

All this started in 1992. It ended ten years later when the government brought in a new immigration law. For the first time Canadian Immigration recognized common law relationships with no gender references.

> **1 (1)** *The definitions in this subsection apply in the Act and in these Regulations.* **Common-law partner** *means, in relation to a person, an individual who is cohabiting with the person in a conjugal relationship, having so cohabited for a period of at least one year. (conjoint de fait)*

"We did it!"

"This crazy group of lesbians and gays sitting around each other's living rooms!"

"It just goes to show that what Margaret Mead said is true!"

> *Never doubt that a small group of thoughtful, committed citizens can change the world; indeed, it's the only thing that ever has.*

Not quite the world. But at least one part of it! Oh, the power of the Internet! On April 30, 1993, the European Organization for Nuclear Research had put the web into the public domain. As a result, word went around the world that Canada was LGBT friendly and that Immigration accepted LGBT people. Many of the emails that we received were from people in countries like Iran, Pakistan, Uganda, Turkey.

"We have so much here in Canada. Our lives are pretty good. We have so many rights now. These people are afraid of being killed!"

"So what are we going to do?"

"What can we do?"

"Well, this is a whole lot different from helping LGBT Canadians with sponsoring their partners."

"Yes, I don't think LEGIT can do refugee stuff, too. Let me talk to a couple of people." I went to talk to the lawyer who had represented me with our court case. As a lawyer who advertised to the LGBT, he acknowledged that he, too, was receiving many emails from people seeking Canada's protection. We organized a meeting and invited community members to come together to see what we could do for all these people experiencing persecution because of their gender identity or sexual orientation. A good place to start. To our surprise almost all the people who showed up were LGBT people here in Canada, afraid to go home to the countries they came from. We listened to them. Eventually everybody left.

"Well, that didn't help us come up with any way to respond to all the emails. We're no further ahead!"

"No, now we have another group of people looking for answers!"

"True. But this is who we had in front of us."

"We have to decide which way to go. We can't do it all!" At least we were smart enough to recognize that!

The lawyer had experience representing asylum seekers at the Immigration and Refugee Board. The way forward seemed clear. Find a way to assist people already here in Canada to be able to stay. We decided that we would start drop-in sessions to provide information about steps people could take so that they didn't have to return home. So the Rainbow Refugee Committee began. It was the year 2000. We recruited several more volunteers who had been part of LEGIT. The drop-ins were very successful. The numbers grew. Every month there were more and more people who came. The meeting room became too small! Every month forty or fifty people, all at different stages of the process, attended. Those who were further ahead in the process shared their experience with those who were waiting. When a member had a successful hearing, they came and shared it with the newer people. The room vibrated with all the clapping.

In 2011, the phone rang. "This is the Minister's office. He would like to talk to you." Two of us went to a phone. "This is Jason Kenney. We want Rainbow Refugee to take on a pilot project to start sponsoring LGBT people escaping persecution." We had come full circle.

Rainbow Refugee Society now helps sponsor LGBT people fleeing persecution and those who have already fled persecution. Members of the LGBT community and allies have sponsored almost 200 members of the LGBT community in Canada. All this began by bringing a small group of people together. Together, we socialized the problems. We found solutions.

Working from the Inside
Farren Gillaspie

Living in a world surrounded by homophobia, I learned early on that it works better for me to enter by the side door, rather than to bust down the front door. I have been in my current job for thirty-six years. I was impressed by the fact that this fledgling, non-profit society stood for the same ideals that I held dear. They promoted equal rights for all. Of course, they meant that for their developmentally disabled children. I felt, well, I too am part of that 'all' (my definition).

I found out that the board was comprised of mostly very devout Christians. I had decided not to lie about my orientation, but I wouldn't volunteer information either. The organization was quite small then, but it quickly grew. The director was very appreciative of my dedication. There were several times when he seemed to be opening the door for me to come out. However, he had never shared anything of his personal life. I knew from other employees he was married and had children. So I just didn't respond. I heard from his assistant one time that he said to her, "What the hang is this guy? I thought he was straight, then I was quite sure he was gay. Now, just the other day, he introduced me to his 17-year-old daughter who was visiting from Quebec! What do you think?"

"I think it's none of our business. He is one of your best employees, so I say stay out of his business," she replied.

A few years in, my assistant came out to me as being HIV positive. I was concerned how the religious families and the HR department would handle this. I thought about that side door. This was the eighties, and the AIDS crisis was at its peak. In a coordinators' meeting with some family members present, I suggested we have an in-service from AIDS Vancouver, so we could better understand how

AIDS might affect our employees. The director was quick to point out that the answer was obvious: a person with a communicable disease cannot work in this environment. I responded, "That is precisely why we need an in-service. HIV is transmitted through sexual activity and needles, etc. which, of course, our staff would not be participating in. But I was thinking of your children. Most of them have been institutionalized for fifteen or sixteen years. We know that sexual abuse had been, unfortunately, fairly common. What if one of your children tested positive for HIV, and their support staff chose not to work with them?"

The in-service came.

A few years later, I put on the agenda for our coordinators' meeting, a question about same-sex benefits for our employees. The answer was quick, "Our carrier would not offer that coverage." I suggested that we formally ask our carrier and bring their response to our next meeting in a month. The carrier's reply came with a flat, "No, not at this time." I had learned a lot from the family members who had advocated for rights for their disabled children getting them out of the institution. Calm, clear persistence and a refusal to accept 'No' always worked for them eventually. Next meeting, I suggested that we send yet another letter to our carrier, this time reminding them that ICBC had been offering same-sex benefits for five years already, and asking if we might consult with them on how we could support our over 350 employees. It was a very slow, aggravating process, but about six months later we had our benefits. This was, of course, not a one-man show. Most of our employees were totally behind the request, and we had some strong representatives in our management team.

One of my staff worked part time at our workplace while earning his law degree. Our agency was upgrading their policies and procedures just as he became a practising lawyer. He was a totally out, very personable, six-foot-two, blond dynamo. I suggested that since he knew our agency, he could present a seminar on respect in the workplace. This would address legal issues around harassment and discrimination based on gender, sexual orientation, race, religion, etc. He did a brilliant presentation that was very balanced. Some board members and some supervisors were squirming, but it was all in line with our labour laws. Many of us breathed a little easier.

My partner passed away in 1997. I went right back to work without any time off. My first day back, I got a call from the director of employee services. She said she had heard my partner had passed and offered her condolences. Then she said, "You know, you are entitled to at least three days of bereavement leave. Why don't you use it? Take the rest of the week off." When I got home that night, there was a beautiful bouquet of flowers outside my condo door. It had a card that was signed by all eleven staff from the administration office, many with touching thoughts below their names.

I was fortunate to meet a very special man four years later, and we have been together for seventeen years. He has attended all of the society celebrations with me. At an awards ceremony two years ago when I was a recipient, we sat at one of many large tables. My partner sat across the table and was talking to the father of one of my residents. A woman sat beside me. She was without a doubt the most staunch Christian on the board. We chatted a bit, then she asked me who the handsome man across the table was. I said, "My partner."

"Really, how long have you been together?"

"Fifteen years."

"That is amazing! I would say it looks like you are two very fortunate men."

I'm Here with You
Cyndia Cole

From 1984 until the millennium, I worked in home support with people who needed health care at home due to age, illness, or disability. Death was a constant in our work world, but there were all kinds of variations on how we handled it.

When the 80 and 90-year-olds left for hospital or facilities and died in care, we usually took it in stride saying, "He had a nice long life," or "Because of our workers, she could get her wish to live at home for as long as possible." We felt we'd done our best and could accept that everyone dies in good time. We hadn't known those folks in their prime. We liked their stories about their younger days, but we didn't have a personal sense of loss seeing someone we'd known as vital and active declining and limited. Their loved ones saw them as 'shadows of their former selves', but we just took them as they were. The clients liked that they had nothing to live up to with us. We never begged them not to go or to be more than they could manage. Those were the expected or 'good deaths' that let us feel our compassion and hard work were all worthwhile.

It wasn't always like that. Mr. Harding committed suicide. His worker, Nathan, and I were deeply shocked. My co-supervisor, Bill, anticipated our spiral into the black hole of guilt and regret. Mr. Harding never once spoke of wanting to kill himself. He wasn't in excruciating pain. He didn't have a debilitating or terminal illness. He was old and frail and about to move from the seniors' residence into the care facility nearby. He didn't express regrets or hesitation. He seemed all set.

Then we learned the day before his move he had pushed a chair to his fourth-floor window, struggled to climb up, and managed to tip himself out onto the cement driveway below. If he'd chosen his other window, he'd have fallen onto the grass and might have survived.

"Why didn't we see it coming? Why didn't we stop him?" Nathan and I asked ourselves and each other as we replayed our every interaction with Mr. Harding. Bill saved me with his wise and experienced perspective. He was so definitive.

"You didn't know because he didn't want you to know. He wanted to succeed, so he gave no signs," Bill said. "If he'd wanted you to stop him, he would have let you see it coming. You couldn't have stopped him. It was what he wanted. You didn't fail him, so let it go." Amazingly, I did let it go and would learn to do the same with the many other 'not good deaths' that would follow.

I think I was able to face the 'not good' deaths because Bill was always there as my friend and co-worker. A young client with schizophrenia jumped off her roof the day she was sent home from psychiatric care. We cursed the system's limited resources and consoled her worker. Our middle-aged worker, Althea, dropped dead of a heart attack walking to her client Orsola's home. Bill ran out to support Orsola, while I spoke with Althea's family. When Orsola, who was much older, was discovered dead in her bed soon after, we took time away from our busy desks and attended her funeral together, doing our Buddhist chant softly and respectfully during the Anglican prayers.

The deaths from AIDS were like a tidal wave. I felt I couldn't resist them, or I'd go under. I could only surf if I surrendered, knowing I was not in control. What I could do was keep my humanity. On Halloween, I dressed up as a Rainbow Clown and made a few rare visits to some of my favourite guys.

Of course, our workers needed training to protect themselves from contracting the HIV virus, and most of all to counteract the hysteria and panic that they would catch homosexuality and die from it. The supervisors attended the first of many sessions offered by AIDS Vancouver held in the cramped basement of our office. Since I knew the information already, I was free to focus on how it was presented. The playful irony of the young lesbian as she showed how to put condoms on a banana made quite an impression. She quizzed us on which bodily fluids might transmit the virus. She kept saying with a smile "You've missed my favourite." It was my favourite too, but I would have outed myself and started laughing if I had named it. How I longed to blow off the need to 'remain professional'. Bill saw me fighting my impulse to be outrageous, so he reined in witty cracks about the banana or favourite fluids, and we both maintained our decorum. We made sure all our workers got to the training sessions.

The turnover in AIDS clients was rapid. They might receive our service for only a few weeks or months before they died. I'm sure Bill and I had at least three hundred within a few years. One who touched me deeply was Daniel, a fellow who had played the organ for his church. He was waiting for his mum to arrive from back east, so she could care for him full time. How hard was it for a thirty-year-old, grown man to be cared for like a baby again? Daniel was lucky to have her because most of the guys were abandoned by all family and completely dependent on other Persons with AIDS (PWA). The PWA were ill, too, and would also die before long.

Daniel's brain was being attacked by infection, and a different part of his body became paralyzed each day. He realized he wasn't going to make it until his mum arrived. He was losing the power of speech as paralysis spread to his throat. Already he couldn't walk and was expected to die within hours, not days. Daniel took the trouble to phone me. He thanked me more sincerely than I had ever been thanked before. I had never met him face to face, and he'd only been a client for a couple of weeks. I felt I had done so little to help him. I asked myself: would I spend my last available words calling a relative stranger to express appreciation? Could I think about someone else's feelings so close to my departure? Could I learn to live with the courage to look death in the face like Daniel and these other young heroes?

Our co-workers whose sons faced death from AIDS also touched me and Bill so poignantly. We understood the gripping fear of stigma. We'd both been victimized by that fear from our youth. Since

Bill had mastered keeping his sexual orientation secret for so long, people just knew their secrets were safe with him. The supervisor, Florence, told everyone else that her brilliant and accomplished son, Douglas, passed from cancer. She trusted me and Bill with the truth. We attended Douglas's funeral together in the West End church where the minister wore a rainbow striped sash over his white robes. I remember that service now when I see this minister as a city councilor. The only other staff there were Mary and her partner, Andrea. They say the pain of losing your child is like no other. Bill and I felt we could reach through the walls Florence tried to build around her sorrow. We tried to hold that pain with tenderness as she let us into her fortress.

Carena's situation was even more delicate. Bill and I were her supervisors. She was struggling at work and confided in us that her son, Theo, was in hospice care in the downtown eastside at May's Place. Carena and Theo were from Grenada in the Caribbean. She felt there was not a soul in her community of immigrants she could share with. She invited Bill and me to Theo's last birthday party. He was turning twenty. I was delighted to find a balloon that became the body of a paper pink flamingo. It would walk a little on the floor as the helium in the balloon bobbed it along. I thought it tropical, possibly evoking home for them as I remembered the pink flamingos living nearby when I was in Florida.

Theo was even taller and thinner than Carena, yet seemed just a younger, gayer version of his mum. Thankfully there were lots of patients, staff, and volunteers at the hospice to join the bright and joyful event. Did this make up for the complete absence of relatives? Another patient who was enjoying himself despite his frailty quipped to me, "I've been living in loneliness on skid row all my life. Why did I have to wait until I'm dying to be in a beautiful, loving place like this?"

I saw Carena by surprise fifteen years later. She'd retired early due to her arthritis. It was reassuring to see her doing well in subsidized housing near Jericho beach. I was there for a health fair in the common room. She insisted I come to her apartment and choose a bag from the many she'd sewed and laid out on her bed. I picked a multi-coloured patchwork one that struck me as Caribbean style. I have it still. It's infused with her undying gratitude that Bill and I saw her secrets and, therefore, her.

On May 23, 2018, I sat in Vancouver City Hall chambers and celebrated the Proclamation of "Year of the Queer." The minister I remembered from Douglas's funeral was chairing as one of his last triumphs before leaving office as City Councillor. Ten speakers told the elected officials and sympathetic friends about their Queer organizations' great contributions to the community. The room was formal and impressive, almost somber, with dark wood. We attendees were far from the rag-taggle outcasts we'd seemed to be so long ago. The speaker from AIDS Vancouver recalled the six men who'd met in a living room thirty-five years before with the vain hope and determination to 'do something' for themselves and others made invisible and abandoned by the gay plague.

I missed the middle part of his speech as I drifted off into memories of Jill's friend, Taavi, who was one of those six heroes. I was jolted back when the speaker said, "Very soon there will be a vaccine preventing anyone from infection, illness, and death from HIV and AIDS." I felt Taavi, Daniel, Douglas, Theo and all the other dearly departed sitting right beside me. And I wept. And in my heart, I said to them and to me, "You won! You won! I'm here with you, so you can know that you won."

If I Had a Hammer: Remembering Christopher Colorado Jones, 70

Don Martin

A dear gay friend and mentor of mine died on the fiftieth anniversary of the Stonewall Inn riots, June 2019. Christopher Colorado Jones was putting up a rainbow flag at his house in San Francisco to commemorate Pride Week when he fell from a ladder and sustained a fatal brain injury. It was a shocking end to an amazing life.

Chris was a radical peace activist from an early age. As a teenager, he refused to register for the draft and go to Vietnam. After several trials, he was sent to prison. At the time of his death, Chris was in the middle of producing a full-length film about his fellow Vietnam draft resisters called "The Boys Who Said NO!" It includes interviews with Joan Baez and David Harris with whom he worked in the '60s and '70s. The film is nearly finished. Chris got to show early cuts of it to fundraising audiences around the country. Many friends have taken an oath to see that the project is completed.

After Chris served his prison sentence in the '70s, he was the director of the Agape Foundation that provided grants to social change organizations. Then he got his degree in public health and helped manage HIV/AIDS prevention efforts at the Northwest AIDS Foundation and the Washington State Department of Health, where he and I were colleagues for a decade.

During the early '90s working in public health, Chris and I were both single, gay men living in the state capital of Olympia, a small town at the southern end of Puget Sound. Outside of work, we saw each other at many social gatherings and even went on a couple of dates. I believe Chris wanted a more serious relationship, but at the time I felt it was important to keep my personal and professional lives separate. Eventually, I met my future husband, John, and Chris warmly embraced us as a couple. Chris even asked John and me to housesit for him while he travelled, one of his great passions. As Chris grew frustrated with small-town life, he decided to move to Seattle where he worked for the state's largest local health department. He met his husband in Seattle, and they eventually moved to San Francisco and travelled the world together.

I know how much Chris meant to his friends and colleagues because of his serious dedication to peace, justice, and various social causes, but I wanted to memorialize my dear friend with a more humourous story. In 1992, a right-wing Christian group in the state of Oregon successfully overturned civil rights protections for state and municipal employees who were gay and lesbian. Then they turned their sights on our state, Washington, where several cities and the state government had similar anti-discrimination protections. The Oregon group was determined to create a popular movement against 'special rights' as they called the basic civil rights of LGBTQ people. I was part of the effort in Washington to fight a proposed initiative which was financed with Oregon money. We called ourselves 'Hands Off Washington'. We organized grassroots efforts in nearly every county in the state. I volunteered to produce a fundraising event in Olympia. I had been doing a lot of theatre and had experience producing revues and musical events.

The fundraiser was based on the old TV show, *The Dating Game*. The original show from the '60s and '70s featured a young, single man or woman, separated by a partition from three potential opposite-sex dates. The idea was to ask revealing questions, often loaded with sexual innuendo and, based on the answers, select one of the three for a date, sight unseen. Our Dating Game, however, was all about same-sex dates. We held it in the town's only gay bar, and all the proceeds went to Hands Off Washington. I recreated the old studio set, complete with a partition, stools, psychedelic lettering, and stylized flowers. I even found the Herb Alpert theme song. We staged it as if it were in front of a studio audience. It was completely unrehearsed. We did two rounds of the game, one with women and one with men.

In place of TV host Jim Lange, I got two members of a popular local singing group, the Righteous Mothers, to emcee. They adopted personas from one of their stage bits, calling themselves the Schnorrer Sisters. I asked a local newspaper columnist to help me write silly questions for the contestants to ask of their prospective dates. One of my favourites was, "If I had a hammer, and you had a bell, what song would we sing all over this land?" And, of course, after the uproarious responses, the Schnorrer Sisters spontaneously broke into song, and we cut to commercial. I had engaged actors from a local theatre group (that was then performing a weekly live soap opera) to do mock commercials in the breaks. In one commercial, two soldiers relaxing in their barracks, cleaning their rifles, promoted a new men's cologne called *Don't Tell*, 'for when you can't ask'. The polishing of gun barrels built to an hysterical climax.

I had enlisted my friend Chris's help in brainstorming possible participants for the game, but we had great difficulty finding single, gay men and lesbians who were willing to risk humiliation and be on stage. Well, actually, it was pretty easy to find willing lesbians. But nearly all the single, gay men we knew refused. They claimed stage fright. I finally convinced an assistant to the state governor to be the celebrity, gay male date. But right up until the day before the event, we only had two male contestants. Of course, I had tried several times to convince Chris to do it. He was an obvious catch: cute, fun-loving, and well-known in the community for his work and for his political commitment to the cause. And it was no secret that he was seeking a boyfriend. "Think of all the men in the audience who will learn you are available," I told him. But he claimed he was too shy. The day before the show, I begged him one last time, saying I would put in a good word to the governor's assistant beforehand. He reluctantly agreed.

Chris answered the silly questions with poise and humour, but when it came time to choose, he wasn't picked. It turned out the governor's assistant knew Chris and one of the other contestants, and despite my urging, he decided to pick the one guy he had never met. Chris wouldn't speak to me for a week.

The fundraiser was a community-building success. We stopped the anti-gay initiative in Washington, and the Oregon anti-gay law was later ruled unconstitutional. LGBTQ rights had some ups and downs in our state after that, but statewide nondiscrimination protections were enacted in 2006, and in 2012 Washington became the first U.S. state to legalize same-sex marriage by popular vote.

QUIRK-E AUTHORS

Marsha Ablowitz, MSW, age 75, worked in community mental health and volunteered in feminist organizations. She started Vancouver's first women's self defense groups, lesbian support groups and incest survivor groups. She did this before these issues became mainstream. Now she has fun hiking, traveling, carving, and writing.

Richard Brail turns 70 this year and wonders how and when that happened. He had two careers, lawyer and librarian. As a lawyer he often represented queers in the criminal and the civil courts as well as before tribunals, and advised gay men on a variety of issues affecting their lives. Over the years he often spoke at conferences, public meetings, and other events about issues affecting the gay community. He and Adrien have recently celebrated 33 years of connubial bliss.

Janie Cawley I would like to think my story reveals the seed of my now strong, independent, rather anti-authoritarian lesbian-feminist self. The seed took a lot of hard knocks before it started to germinate. I had to get married to really find out what most men's idea of women's role in the world was. I had to leave the marriage to gain my independence and proclaim my feminist beliefs. I had only to experience the friendship of a group of strong lesbian-feminist women to discover my true orientation. I discovered 'real' women. I came out as a lesbian. The seed came into full bloom in 1982.

Cyndia Cole moved from the USA to Vancouver in 1970 and came out as a lesbian at age 26 in 1976. Her writing appears in *Basically Queer: An Intergenerational Introduction to LGBTQA2S+ Lives, Making Room: Forty Years of Room Magazine, Sharing Our Journeys* and *Breakthrough*. Daisaku Ikeda taught her that words change people's hearts. She is honoured to have worked with others to found or develop Women's Studies at SFU, Vancouver East Housing Co-op, humanistic Home Support, Quirk-e, QMUNITY and SGI Vancouver Buddhist Pride Group.

Judy Fletcher is 73. Her mother often described her ersatz curly headed youngest as 'queer duck'. Judy was not offended because she knew she was different. Rural Ontario didn't provide any gay, lesbian, or trans role models either on television or out in the community. Judy grew into the 'queer' label but didn't understand why she was a duck. She doesn't even like the water.

Sheila Gilhooly As a butch dyke for the last fifty years, my right to be in women's spaces like washrooms has been challenged frequently. Even with picture ID, confrontations with gatekeepers and officials have been pretty consistently threatening and humiliating. Writing these stories has connected me to allies fighting for the same right to belong. The transgender activism of the last twenty years has decreased the frequency and hostility of these confrontations, and changed their tone. These days I am more likely to get an apology than a threat.

Farren Gillaspie is 67 and lives in Vancouver with his partner of 17 years. He came from humble beginnings on an Ontario farm and escaped when he was 17. His stories reflect his queer journey from youthful awakening through family tragedy and celebration.

River Glen feels like Quirk-e is so much more than a writing group. As the years pass, we are a pillar in the queer community. We support each other, other queer organizations, and help further queer culture. Our work is both individual and collaborative, reflective and proactively shaping our now. My senior years are greatly enriched by this group I call family.

Dr. Stephen Hardy is Métis and two-spirited. He has a PhD in Electrical Engineering from the University of Alberta. He was a professor at a number of universities in western Canada, including Universities of Saskatchewan, Regina, UBC, and SFU. He was the Director of Electrical Research at the Saskatchewan Power Corporation R&D Centre and Executive Director of the BC Microelectronics Society. He has retired to a position of Professor Emeritus at Simon Fraser University.

Pat Hogan, 80, has been an activist and organizer in the feminist and LGBTQA2S+ communities since the mid 1970s. She supports the plethora of identifying words used in the queer community while proudly holding on to her lesbian roots. Family, friends, travel, dance, reading, and writing enrich her life.

Greta Hurst is 83. "My Early Years in School" describes how venturing from home to school was about meeting the world for the first time. "Getting Old" describes me today with lots of memories from my past life, but recent memories that leave me almost as soon as I experience them. Life is still exciting and fun, so if the gods are willing, I have many more years yet.

Val Innes, 73, is retired from university teaching with more time to spend travelling, painting, and writing. She's a lesbian feminist and activist who has worked at making the world a better, more equal place, both personally and professionally, since the '70s, teaching, volunteering, organizing, writing, and protesting to help bring about positive change. Her writing appears in ***Basically Queer***: *An Intergenerational Introduction to LGBTQA2S+ Lives, Sharing Our Journeys,* several Quirk-e anthologies, and *I Want to Meet You There.*

Don Martin has been a feminist, antiwar, and LGBTQ activist since the late 1960s. He started one of the first gay organizations for college students in Washington state in 1972. Don co-founded Hard Rain Printing Collective (1975 – 1984), a worker-run printing/publishing business, and was a playwright and performer in the street theatre troupe called Theatre of the Unemployed (1974 – 1986). He has since acted, directed, sung, and designed sets in more than fifty theatrical productions. He joined Quirk-e in 2016 after retiring from a career in public health education and becoming a permanent Canadian resident in 2014.

Chris Morrissey is a 76-year-old, White lesbian. Her partner of 40 years, Bridget, died after living with dementia for several years. Together they worked with others to change Canada's immigration legislation to recognize same-sex relationships as family. Their family expanded when they were adopted as grammas, a role they loved.

Nora D Randall is a writer and storyteller. She and Jackie Crossland formed Random Acts (1988-2000) to tell the stories of lesbians and working women. She joined Quirk-e in 2018.

Gayle Roberts is a 78-year-old retired high school teacher who transitioned from male to female on the job twenty years ago. Since her transition, Gayle has actively supported transitioning children, adolescents, and adults. She is co-author of the guidebook *Supporting Transgender and Transsexual Students* in K-12 schools.

Lari Souza, 23, is a proud feminist trans man who was born in Brazil but moved to India in his adolescent years. Since 2015, Lari has made Vancouver his home. He is a youth volunteer with Quirk-e and is currently completing a Bachelor's degree in International Studies and Gender, Sexuality and Women's Studies at Simon Fraser University. Lari's mission is to bring peace, justice, and happiness to the community through his writings, Buddhist practice, and his passion for cooking.

Nancy Strider The safety and encouragement of Quirk-e supports Nancy's articulation, at age 67, of her asexual identity. For ten years, the group has provided a home for her creative work. After initially connecting as host artist for digital imaging, she committed to membership, gaining skills in writing and performing.

Paula Stromberg, 68, collaborates with artists to communicate efforts to address women's empowerment and human rights issues, including same-sex marriage. Exploring queer difference can challenge care structures in society including gender oppressions, international conversation about economic systems, and our approach to the ruling class of elites—ideas that could energize the next wave of queer activism.

Harris Taylor is a 59-year-old writer and documentary filmmaker who has contributed programming to Vision TV, CBC, and Northern Native Broadcasting in the Yukon. Where mainstream media have often failed issues of social justice, Quirk-e has allowed Harris to tell stories that triumph over homophobia.

Ellen Woodsworth is an international urban consultant on intersectional planning and was the first out lesbian city councillor in Canada. Chairperson of Woman Transforming Cities (which partnered in authoring the *Advancing Equity and Inclusion Guide for Municipalities*), she hosted a queer consultation that created the Queer Declaration calling for inclusion in the New Urban Agenda of UN Habitat 3.

GUEST ARTISTS

Dorothy Dittrich is an award-winning playwright, musical director, sound designer, and composer. Her plays include *The Piano Teacher, Mouthpiece, When the Moon Falls, The Dissociates*, and the musical *When We Were Singing*. She has been commissioned by Arts Club Theatre, Kay Meek Theatre, Kickstart Disability Arts & Culture, and Sea Theatre. She was a writer in residence at Buddies in Bad Times in Toronto. Her work has garnered the Sydney J. Risk Award, Jessies, and nominations for the Dora Award.

Sarah Leavitt is the author of the graphic memoir *Tangles: A Story About Alzheimer's, My Mother, and Me*, published in Canada, the US, UK, Germany, France, and Korea. It was a finalist for the Writers' Trust Non-Fiction Prize in 2010, and is currently in development as a feature-length animation. Her new book, *Agnes, Murderess*, is horror/historical fiction set in 19th-century British Columbia. She teaches comics classes at the University of British Columbia.

Claire Robson has authored two books, *Love in Good Time*, a memoir, and *Writing for Change*, a text on memoir as community activism, and has co-edited **Basically Queer** *An Intergenerational Introduction to LGBTQA2S+ Lives,* as well as four other anthologies. Her short stories and poetry have appeared in many literary journals. Her research, which is ongoing, investigates the capacity of arts practices to build community, navigate identity, and generate social change.